Torah Today

For out of Zion shall come forth
Torah and the word of the Almighty
from Jerusalem.
Isaiah 2:2

And these words which I command you today
shall be upon your heart.
Deuteronomy 6:6

. . . they should always be as if you heard them
today, always fresh, always new.
Talmud

Jewish History, Life, and Culture
MICHAEL NEIDITCH, SERIES EDITOR

Torah Today

A Renewed Encounter with Scripture

Pinchas H. Peli

With a new foreword by Harold M. Schulweis

University of Texas Press
Austin

This book has been supported by
The Jewish History, Life, and Culture Series endowment
funded by Milton T. and Helen G. Smith and the Moshana Foundation,
and the Tocker Foundation.

Illustrations by Phillip Ratner. His multimedia works appear in permanent
collections of museums and synagogues throughout the world. Realizing the
dream of his life, Mr. Ratner founded the Israel Bible Museum in Safad, Israel.

Requests for permission to reproduce material from this work should be sent to
Permissions, University of Texas Press, Box 7819, Austin, TX 78713-7819.

∞ The paper used in this book meets the minimum requirements of
ANSI/NISO Z39.48-1992 (R1997) (Permanence of Paper).

Library of Congress Cataloging-in-Publication Data

Peli, Pinchas.
   Torah today : a renewed encounter with scripture / Pinchas H. Peli ; with a
new foreword by Harold M. Schulweis.— 2nd ed.
      p.   cm. — (Jewish life, history, and culture)
   Originally published: Washington, D.C. : B'nai B'rith Books ; [Silver Spring,
Md.] : Published and distributed by Information Dynamics, c1987.
   Includes index.
   ISBN 0-292-70672-3 (pbk. : alk. paper)
   1. Bible. O.T. Pentateuch—Meditations.   I. Title.   II. Series.
   BS1225.54.P45 2005
   222'.106—dc22   2004017742

Contents

For our children and grandchildren.
Isaiah 59:21

Torah Today Week by Week

Foreword
Dialogue with Torah
HAROLD M. SCHULWEIS

TWO SACRED TEXTS are cradled in the lecterns of the synagogue: the Siddur and the Chumash, the Prayer Book and the Five Books of Moses. Prayer and study are the twin modes of Jewish worship.

At the end of each synagogue service, my grandfather would walk up and down the aisle to close the Bibles and prayer texts left open by the worshippers. When once I asked him the reason for his self-appointed ritual, he explained that, just as one does not abruptly break off a conversation with a friend, one should not abandon the texts without proper closure. We engage the texts in dialogue, and to walk away from them without a proper farewell is disrespectful.

The texts of prayer and study are vertical and horizontal conversations between the contemporary congregation and its inherited tradition. Sacred texts are reciprocal dialogues between the revealed and the received. Whatever is revealed must be filtered, whatever is transmitted calls for interpretation. Unopened, the gift of Torah (*Mattan Torah*) is like an unopened letter. The gift must be accepted and received (*Kabbalat Torah*).

Pinchas Peli's learned commentaries are informed by

the variety of interpretation from a tradition that embraces rationalistic and mystical voices. As he writes, "There are seventy faces to the Torah, and the seventy become seven hundred or more. There was always a 'new face' when one reads the portion and it was always fascinating and enthralling." Peli's commentaries offer a fresh face that enlivens the Torah.

Commentary frees the text from literalist rigidity. The narration of the Torah is not only about what has happened "then and there," but also about what is happening "now and here." The revelation is old and new, revealing the mind of an ancient community and the inner recesses of the present self.

Peli's commentaries not only revere the past, but also respect the present. If God's name, YHWH, is a conflation of past-present-future tenses (*Hayah, Hoveh, Yihyeh*), his commentaries reflect the three tenses of our collective and individual lives.

The Torah requires "hearing," and for Peli this means that there is more to the Torah than "doing." Consider his insightful commentaries on Exodus 24, verse 7 (Mishpatim), in which the Israelites respond to the revealed Word of God by declaring: "All that the Lord has spoken we will do and we will hear." (*Na'aseh v'nishmah*.) Behavior appears to antedate understanding. It suggests the priority and primacy of "doing."

But Peli, like his mentor Abraham Joshua Heschel, is disturbed by the bifurcation that splits behavior from belief, and that tends to turn the polarity of Halachah and Aggadah into oppositional polarization. Like Heschel, Peli is wary of those philosophers such as Spinoza, Moses Mendelssohn, and Yeshayahu Leibovitz, who see Judaism not as a way of thought, belief, and opinion, but solely as a way of being. They have reduced Judaism to obedience, to blind submission to a discipline of "doing" alone.

Peli challenges the priority and primacy of "doing," fully aware that religious behaviorism often degenerates into a mechanical ritualization and routinization of the spiritual life. So we find Peli arguing that "doing and hearing" are not discrete imperatives, separate mandates. They are one and the same thing, and the verse should be rendered: "We will do and hear, hearing as we do, and doing as we hear simultaneously." Peli buttresses his position by reminding the reader that God has previously prepared Israel for the Revelation by saying, in Exodus 19:5 (Yithro), "And now, if you will hear My voice, and keep My covenant, then you shall be My treasured possession among all the people."

To hear is to understand. The *Shema* urges the reader and the worshipper to understand what he is to do. The Divine Commander does not issue orders to be blindly obeyed. A vast amount of Midrashic material frequently imagines the dialogue of dissent between Israel's leaders and God. Religious dissent is based upon the hearing of the heart and mind, which is encouraged by the Commander.

Reviewing the commentaries of Peli, I am drawn to a powerful metaphor from a rabbinic Midrash, which understands the Torah to be like a mirror. The mirror is one, but whoever looks at it sees his own face reflected. There is no immaculate perception. Commentaries offer testimony to the magnificent pluralistic perspectivalism of Judaism.

Peli's insights reflect his own honesty and modesty. His wide erudition is evident, but he knows that his is not the only and last word, but an invitation to look at the words of others and, equally important, to look within. If the Torah as the mirror is one, the reflections are many. Wisdom urges that we compare our reflections, lest we are caught in the web of idolatry which sees my reflection as the only true interpretation.

Peli's concluding commentary observes that, in the Book of Joshua, God says to Joshua, the successor of Moses, "My servant Moses is dead." Peli asks, "Did not Joshua know this?" He answers that the Voice was meant for Joshua, to remind him that one cannot go back nor yearn for the leadership of the deceased Moses. No leader and no commentary are to be deified. One must revere the past without ignoring the sanctity of the present.

The eternity of Torah is assured through its internality. So many of the Jewish commentaries, rabbinic and Chasidic, are intrapersonal. The entire Torah can be read on multiple levels—between God and man, between man and man, and between man and self. (*Bayn Adam L'atzmo.*) Consider what it does for the reader to translate the Ten Commandments as intrapersonal mandates: e.g., not to steal from oneself, not to kill oneself, not to bear false witness against oneself, not to covet oneself. The reflexive mode opens a new vein to carry fresh blood to the heart of Judaism. The commentary on Torah expresses the vitality of the eternal, internal people who would not preserve the text through cryogenic storage. Through commentary, the Torah enjoys the immortality of influence, as does the author of this book.

Preface

WHEN A COLLEAGUE SUGGESTED that this book be subtitled "a contemporary midrash," I felt it would be presumptuous for me to appropriate as revered a concept such as midrash which comes from another era, another world. Midrash constitutes one of the high points in the formation of the Jewish classical literary heritage. No one can write a "Bible," nor compose a "Talmud" or a "Midrash" without risking the sin of parody, or at best, poor imitation. The essays collected in this book do, however, represent a conscious attempt to follow and emulate the traditional midrash, not only as a certain specific literary genre, but also in the way the midrash responds to the ever-renewed encounter with Torah.

There are numerous connotations of the word "Torah" in biblical as well as in post-biblical, even modern, Hebrew. It is used here both as referring to the Pentateuch (the first five books of Scripture) and also to the sum-total of the "teaching" (that is indeed the etymological derivation of the word) of Judaism on the essence of life and how to live it. This teaching identified itself as embracing the word of God the supreme Teacher (*ha-melamed torah*— "the One who teaches Torah"— is an epithet of God in

Jewish liturgy), along with all other "teachings" gleaned from Torah that conscientious disciples in every generation "heard" and learned from the "Teacher" in their innermost being.

Torah was passed on to posterity, not as closed, boxed-in wisdom, but as open-ended, ongoing conversation, originating in the eternal encounter between the will and word of God and the people of Israel (and through them to all humanity), throughout their historical vicissitudes.

The event at Sinai may have been a one-time historical event, but the act of Revelation, the revealing of the truths of Torah, never ceases.

By tuning in and responding to the encounter with Torah, we recreate the experience of "hearing" the divine voice. Jewish tradition ensured this permanent encounter by establishing the cyclical weekly reading of a "portion" of Torah, the so-called *parashat ha-shavua*, "the portion of the week." Every week and its "portion." Every Sabbath the entire congregation, not only scholars or saints, is called to a rendezvous with the Teacher, as he emerges from the words of Scripture.

This weekly rendezvous is not a one-sided performance where the audience sits and listens passively and then goes home. The very first act of Revelation at Sinai was not like this either. God did not address his commandments to the children of Israel in the wilderness before entering into a lengthy dialogue with them. (See the essay *Blind Obedience Is Not Enough,* pages 75–79.)

The community, as well as each individual person within it, does not come to this weekly encounter with God's word empty-handed, awe-stricken, and speechless in the presence of the Almighty. The setting is not that of a mighty king issuing orders to his subjects in the form of a solemn royal edict, but rather that of a concerned and wise teacher whose pupils are expected to be ever alert, questioning, probing and debating every word and idea.

It is precisely this encounter that turns God's word into "Torah."

The word Torah, as said before, comes from the same root as the word "moreh" or "morah", meaning a teacher (male or female) in spoken Hebrew. God, the giver of the Torah, is the master teacher; we are the pupils. Torah is constantly recreated and revitalized as a result of this interaction between teacher and pupils.

We bring with us to the "classroom," which springs into being whenever and wherever Torah is studied, the full dimension of our being. We ask questions and search for answers. All questions are allowed, even encouraged. New insights emerge from the encounter with the text which yields more than one answer to any one question. "The Torah has seventy faces," said the ancient rabbis. If one looks hard enough, one finds the face he is seeking.

God spoke once, but that once is always. With the help of the method of midrash we are able to hear it again today. Every day. That is why midrash became one of the most important words in the vocabulary of Jewish life and religion—it teaches us to "hear" ever new "sounds" within the one everlasting voice.

The sages who created the midrash did not come empty-handed to their encounter with Torah. On the contrary, they brought with them all their human experience and accumulated wisdom, their doubts and pains, their wanderings and wonderings. This encounter resulted in renewed understanding, in new insights surfacing as direct replies to immediate questions. The art of midrash consists in the ability to pour old wine into new, contemporary vessels, to transplant some ancient divinely inspired secrets of struggle and joy, and celebration of time and life, into our own limited, often dismal, situations.

Midrash is the link that ties together the chain of being

first perceived in the Bible and continuing up to this very day. What would the world have been like without it? At times, it seems that the instant this chain was severed, there would be no more world; that continuing to listen to this divine-human conversation, which began with the pronouncement of the words "In the beginning God created heaven and earth," is vital to our very existence today, an existence in dire need of a "beginning" and an "end," a destiny and a destination, a meaning beyond absurdity.

A modest contribution to this kind of listening to Torah, today, is offered in the following essays. Ours may not be a generation of towering giants in the study of Torah, but we are nevertheless a link in the same chain. It would be false humility to claim that our generation is spiritually barren and has nothing whatsoever to add to the eternal, ongoing Torah conversation. We may indeed be "midgets" as compared to earlier generations of "giants," but as "midgets riding on the shoulders of giants" our vistas are enormous. We are in the privileged, albeit awe-filled, position of living in a time when we can reap the fruit of the labor of many a genius in the physical sciences as well as in the realm of the human spirit and social vision.

In the Jewish world too we are in possession, as never before, of many of the great treasures of the wisdom of the past. Libraries and bookstores abound in what used to be classified as "rare editions" limited only to the privileged few. Precious spiritual and intellectual treasures are now within the reach of all.

We are the direct heirs of some of the most exciting periods of Jewish living and spiritual creativity. We are chronologically, post-enlightenment-centered worldly *maskilim*, post-piety-centered mystical *hassidim* and post-study-centered rational *mitnagdim*. Historically, we are the immediate survivors of the Holocaust and witnesses to the living miracle of Israel reborn.

Rarely have people lived in a time of such heightened historical and spiritual tension.

Such as we are, our generation again encounters Torah. Some of us are fascinated by it, not only by way of getting to know the past out of scholarly curiosity or nostalgic yearnings, but primarily by way of asking in all candor: what does Torah have to tell us *today?*

We come to this encounter as open-minded people of our time, yet fully aware that we were not born today, nor were we suddenly parachuted from nowhere onto a desert island. We are aware that behind us are three thousand years of living with Torah and its teachings and that there are unfathomable fountains of insightful wisdom, fascinating cultural achievements, and enlightening moral guidance which we might draw from that rich heritage.

Shelves upon shelves of Torah commentaries, the products of the best minds of the Jews for many generations, await our acquaintance, but, alas, they all have their backs turned toward us! What are the secrets they hold? What is the nature of the warmth they exude? Shall we try to find out? And if we do, would it be possible to apply some of it to our own lives?

The sages of the midrash tried to answer these questions in their time; we would like to try in our own small way to try doing it in ours. Aware of the tremendous gap that stretches between our meager strivings and the possible results, we nevertheless keep on trying.

Our efforts may be classified as both "exegesis" and "eisigesis," namely, reading *out* of the text and also *into* it, while drawing on all the resources at our disposal— ancient as well as medieval and modern. Our aim, though, is clear: relating to Torah as it speaks *to us, today.*

The essays presented herewith are based on a weekly column under the name *Tora Today* published during

1984-5 in both the local and international editions of *The Jerusalem Post*. The hundreds of letters that reached the *Post* and the author from all corners of the world, from Jews and non-Jews alike, are proof that people today in every walk of life seek the word of Torah. When the "Guide to Values and Topics" of this book was composed (with the technical help of Rabbi Baruch Gold, my assistant at the Blechner Chair for Jewish Values at Ben Gurion University of the Negev), I was, as some readers may also be, amazed to discover how many and how varied are the values and issues covered in only *one* annual cycle of Torah reading. It confirmed the saying of the second-century sage Ben Bag Bag: "Keep turning to it [Torah] again and again, because everything is in it." (*Mishna Avot* 5, 28).

The weekly burden of meticulous study of the *parasha*, consulting scores of commentaries, the selection of the topic for the week and the attempt to share it with others, writing in a way that would nevertheless appear as "light reading" befitting a daily newspaper, was no easy task. I cannot say however, that it was not a pleasurable task. The letters and phone calls of so many readers were most encouraging, and I would like to take this opportunity to thank them all for their kindness and interest. I also wish to apologize for not replying personally to the much-appreciated correspondence.

It is particularly a joyful task to acknowledge the active participation and contribution of ideas emerging from Torah discussions with my wife and family and numerous guests, Jews and non-Jews, around our Sabbath table. I am grateful to our mind-probing son Avraham Deuel, as well as to our gifted and learned daughters and sons-in-law—Bitha and Dov Harshefi, Emuna and Benyamin Elon, Batsheva and Gilead Seri—and my marvelous grandchildren.

I cannot conceive of this work being accomplished without the constant involvement of my wife and life's partner Penina Peli, who was the first reader and editor of the following chapters. Her own comments on the Torah portion of the week were broadcast year-round every Friday on the English language radio program of the Voice of Israel from Jerusalem.

The editors of *The Jerusalem Post* Erwin Frankel and Ari Rath and the members of its editorial staff, especially Joe Blumberg, Douglas Davis, David Gross, Sasha Sadan and Hanan Sher, deserve special thanks for helpful and friendly cooperation in first bringing *Tora Today* to tens of thousands of readers throughout the world. Robert Bleiweiss, president of Bleiweiss Communications in Calabassas, California, Aliza Yunick and Cybil Kaehimker of Ben-Gurion University, and Raihanna Zaman of Cornell University, all deserve thanks for their technical help during the various stages of the preparation of the manuscript for publication. Thanks are also due to Rabbi Israel C. Stein of Bridgeport, Conn. and Dr. Faezeh Foroutan of Washington, D.C. for their careful and sensitive corrections.

I am grateful to the Almighty for having granted me a share in His Torah enabling me to write these columns at a time in my life when it was most meaningful for me. Writing *Tora Today* every week prompted, and even forced me at times, to set aside—in spite of many obstacles—time for learning. Thanks to *Tora Today*, I gained some wonderful new friends who have been instrumental in publishing this book. Foremost among them is Dr. Michael Neiditch, the resourceful director of the Commission on Continuing Jewish Education of B'nai B'rith International. For Robert Teitler, president of Information Dynamics, publishing significant Jewish books is not merely a business venture but a labor of love. The friendship and cooperation of the renowned artist Phillip Ratner came also thanks to his enthusiastic response to *Tora Today*.

And finally a note on the translation of biblical quotations in the following pages. Many different translations, ancient and contemporary, were regularly consulted. None of them however was exclusively or faithfully followed. The deciding factor in choosing an English rendition was always the original Hebrew text, often as I understood it with the help of the traditional commentaries.

Pinchas Hacohen Peli

בְּרֵאשִׁית
GENESIS

philip ratner

וַיֵּלְכוּ שְׁנֵיהֶם יַחְדָּו

they went both of them together.

Genesis 22:8

A Weekly Renewal

WHEN MY GRANDFATHER wrote a letter or jotted down an appointment, there was only one way he would note down the date: the first, second or third day in the "Life of Sarah," or in "Jethro," or in "Ye shall be holy." These are some of the titles of the weekly portions of the five books of the Torah read in the synagogue each Sabbath of the year.

As the days of the week have no names in Hebrew but are referred to as *yom rishon*, the first day towards the Sabbath, *yom sheni*, the second day towards the Sabbath, and so on, so also the traditional way to refer to the week is by the Torah portion read on its Sabbath.

In my grandfather's generation, as among many Jews today, everybody knew, in any given week, what the portion was. Everybody also knew that the entire reading of the Pentateuch is completed on Simhat Torah (the holiday which immediately follows Succot) and that on the very same day one commences the Torah reading anew, starting again from the beginning. The cycle of the year is identical with the cycle of its weekly Torah readings.

The first Sabbath following Succot is called Shabbat Bereshit. It is the Sabbath which tells of the beginning of creation, and it marks the beginning of the cycle of Torah portions read weekly throughout the year.

The weekly reading of the Torah has never been confined to synagogue ritual, nor was it limited to the Sabbath. It accompanied every Jew, young and old, scholars and ordinary folks alike, throughout the week. One lived with it every day of the year as one lives with the daily sunrise and sunset. The season turned cold and snowy when "Miketz" or "Vayigash" were read and it became hot when "Shoftim" or "Re'eh" came around. One knew that Spring was here when the portions of the book of Leviticus approached.

The text read remained always the same. One is not allowed to change an iota in the written Torah. Yet, in the eyes of the readers it never seemed old or repetitious, antiquated or dated. Every year, as the reading of the new week came around, it looked and tasted new and fresh. There were always new insights found in the text as the flow of new translations and commentaries never ceased.

"There are," said the rabbis, "seventy faces to the Torah." And that seventy became seven hundred and more. There was always a "new face" when one read the portion, and it was always fascinating and enthralling.

A few hundred years ago, a man wrote a book which contained no less than 913 different interpretations of *Bereshit*, the first word of the Torah. He stopped at nine hundred and thirteen because that is the numerical value of the word according to the system of *Gematria*, b=2, r=200, a=1, sh=300, i=10 and t=400, totaling 913.

Readers of the Torah were never bothered by the simpleton's question, which is often shared by the so-called "scientific mind": Of all the commentaries, which is the "true" or "real" one? They knew, as keen students of hermeneutics and modern literary criticism know, that what differentiates great literature from its lesser counterpart is that the former can be interpreted on many levels, all equally "true" and "real." And what is true of great literature is certainly true of the word of God, embodied in Torah.

The rabbis liken it to a letter from a loved one who has gone on a long journey. In our longing for the absent beloved, how many times do we read and re-read that letter; how much meaning do we read into it; and how many different interpretations of every word come to our minds with every new reading!

The Torah is the letter which our lover left us before he departed for far away, where we can have no direct contact with him. Our only way to be with him is to read and re-read the letter. We do this every Sabbath as we read a portion of the Torah. If we are lucky we hear him and sense him again and again, always new, always fresh.

Each week provides us not only with a new text, but also with a new experience. The content of the portion read becomes part of the household for that week. The Torah reading was never the sole province of scholars or rabbis. Everyone had a share of it according to his own level.

The vast literature of the Midrash, with its popular commentaries, parables and stories, was created by rabbis and preachers who taught the portion to the masses over a period of 1,000 years (between around 300 BCE and 700 CE). This activity was continued afterwards by the great medieval Torah commentators Saadia, Rashi, Ibn Ezra, Rashbam, Nahmanides and many others, and during the following centuries, in popular works written in languages spoken by Jews in their dispersion.

What the anthology *M'Am Loez* was for hundreds of years for the Ladino-speaking Jewish communities, the *Tsena Ure'ena* was for those who spoke Yiddish. These books brought the message and insights of the Torah into every home. The latter work, which became especially identified as a book to be read by women, was printed in no less than two hundred ten editions.

In introducing the book to the English reader (currently in a new translation), its publisher, Reb Meir Holder, describes the place of this Yiddish book in the life of the Eastern European shtetel:

"Snatching a tranquil hour from her chores, our pious great-grandmother in the Old Country would seek her favorite nook between the cradle and the fireplace, and open up the well-thumbed "Tzennarenneh" (as the Hebrew title was pronounced in Yiddish) with its familiar woodcuts. Straightening her lace kerchief, she would settle down to follow the fortunes of the children of Israel in ancient times by reading from its careworn pages about the weekly portion of the Torah.

"She shared the anguish of Sarah over Isaac's near-sacrifice; she humbly aspired to the selflessness of the Mother Rachel; she shed an innocent tear for young Joseph in the scorpions pit; shuddered over the grim details of the Egyptian bondage; exulted with Miriam at the crossing of the Red Sea; and found solace for the daily trials of *golus* (exile) in contemplating the spiritual rewards with which the matriarchs of the past together with the faithful mothers of all generations are blessed in the world to come."

The languages in which the Torah is interpreted, as well as the style in which it is done, may have changed radically in recent generations. What does not change, however, is the role of the portion of the week as a source of eternally renewed inspiration and guidance for all.

The Noahide Laws

IT IS HARD to think of a more elating and majestic story in world literature than the biblical story of Creation. From the moment God proclaims, "Let there be light" to the entrance of the Sabbath, the compact tale is resplendent with joy of creativeness and bliss. Following each day of creation is the affirmation that "God saw that it was good," which changes at the conclusion of the six days of creation to "God saw that it was *very* good." The peaceful rest of the Sabbath then comes into the world soon after man and woman appear on the scene.

A psalm, a song unto the day of the Sabbath, is in the air. It does not take long, however, for this idyllic state to be brutally disrupted and the following chapters bring us into the tragic reality, not only of existential human condition, but of God Himself.

The verses appearing at the beginning of the sixth chapter of *Genesis* are indeed terrifying and have haunted me since my childhood: "And the Lord saw how man's wickedness on the earth had become and that every inclination of the thoughts of his heart was only evil all the time. The Lord was grieved that he had made man on the earth, and his heart was filled with sadness."

7

What an awful summation of the state of Man and God, who had only just now entered the scene full of light, joy and expectation! What a terrible picture of a God whose heart is filled with pain and sadness! How did He get himself into this situation? He that is omnipotent and omniscience; He that could easily get himself cheered up calling in the best entertainers, musicians and performers in the world (He is God, He can do anything. He can get everything He wants, can't He?).

Indeed, only a biblical empathetic God, who is inextricably involved in human affairs, can be thus described. Certainly not the god of the philosophers, nor for that matter, the one of common popular conception.

And then, amidst this grim description, and after it seems that all is lost and ready to fall apart, after the Lord says (*verse 7*): "I will wipe mankind whom I have created from the face of the earth, men and animals, and creatures that move along the ground, and birds of the air"— suddenly, a ray of light: "And Noah found favor in the eyes of the Lord" (*verse 8*). The world will not fall apart, it will survive nevertheless, it will be saved because of a single person. Noah. A righteous person.

Midway between Adam and Abraham, after the holocaust of the deluge, the world which God created gets another chance. A new page is opened. There is a smile again on the face of God. "The Lord smelled the pleasing aroma and said in his heart: Never again will I curse the ground because of man, even though every inclination of his heart is evil from childhood, and never again will I destroy all living creatures, as I have done. As long as the earth endures, seedtime and harvest, cold and heat, summer and winter, day and night will never cease" (*Chapter 8:21–22*).

As if the world was created again at this very moment, this time in a covenant with mankind, the first covenant is made with all of humanity, referred to in rabbinic literature as "B'nai Noah," children of Noah, from whom all humans are descended.

It will take another ten generations until Abraham makes another, more specific, covenant with God which will mark the beginning of the Jewish people, chosen as a special task force from among the peoples of the earth.

Whatever that covenant stipulates is binding on all human beings, Jews included—as "there is nothing which is permitted for Jews and prohibited for non-Jews." On the contrary, there is much which is enjoined on Jews and not on non-Jews. The number of precepts for Jews is put at 613; for "children of Noah," at only seven: they must avoid (1) idol worship, (2) incest, (3) murder, (4) blasphemy, (5) theft, (6) injustice to other men, and (7) eating flesh cut from a living animal.

These seven precepts, derived from Scripture and enumerated in the Talmud (*Sanhedrin 56a–b*) are also known as the Noahide Laws and are looked upon as the basic universal law as seen from the point of view of Torah. If God is, as He is in the Bible, the Creator of all human beings, he could not have cared only for Israel and instructed them exclusively in the way of living. The Torah (which means: instruction) that tells us about the creation by God of the entire universe, surely includes also guidance for all God's creatures. This guidance is presented in the Noahide Laws which comprise the essential moral requirements for survival of individual and society.

While the Torah evolves as the particular instruction for Israel, against its specific historic and geographic background, it also sets the required condition for those who seek inclusion in the Noahide covenant of all human beings. Furthermore, salvation or "a share in the world to come," is not limited to the Jews or those who join them, who have to live by the 613 commandments, but is offered equally to non-Jews who adhere to the seven precepts of the "children of Noah."

The gates are open for those who wish to convert and accept the full history and religion of Israel, but it was never the goal of Judaism to make the entire world Jewish. Early Christians, says Rabbi Eliyahu Benamozegh, (1822–1900) who wrote extensively on Noahism, not having understood this point, saw only one of two ways, either the whole world would accept the full Torah, or, failing this, the Jews, in order to make their divine message universal, would have to give up their adherence to Torah. They chose to propagate the latter.

Thus the universal message the world got from Judaism until now was, in the formulation of historian Arnold Toynbee, either in the form of *Christian* Judaism or *Moslem* Judaism, both of which tainted its pure concepts of Monotheism.

The world is still waiting, Toynbee argues, for the universal message of *Judaic* Judaism. This is to be sought in the idea and content of the Covenant and the seven laws of Noah.

In Quest of an Ideal

"NOW THE LORD said to Abraham, Get thee out of thy country, and from thy kindred, and from thy father's house, unto a land that I will show thee" (*Genesis: 12:1*). This is where the biblical story really begins. All that we have read until now were merely broad strokes of pre-historic episodes, setting the stage for the appearance of the major character. Even when we get to Abraham, the hero whom we are going to accompany from now on in great detail, we are kept almost in the dark as to the first seventy-five years of his life. There is a brief reference (*11:31*) to Abraham's family, headed by his father Terah, taking a journey to the land of Canaan, but never making it, as they get stuck in Haran. (Are they the first *noshrim*, as the drop-outs *en route* to Israel are called now?) The real, detailed story of the Bible, however, does not start until the call addressed directly to Abraham: leave your country, your family, your home, and go to a land yet unknown. This call is destined to play a central role in the drama to be acted out between God and Israel.

Professor Andre Neher, draws our attention to the fact that the Hebrew Bible also closes 1,500 years later on the same note of going up to the Promised Land (*II Chronicles*

11

36:23): "Whosoever there is among you of all His people—
the Lord his God be with him—let him go up."

For the people of Israel, the immanence of God in this
world is inextricably linked with the Land. The call addressed to Abraham to go to the Land is so meaningful
that anything which happened in his life up to this point
(and on which Jewish Midrashism and the Islamic Koran
elaborate) is totally ignored. This juncture is of fundamental significance in the entire biblical story.

In the words of one of the most renowned modern Bible scholars, E.A. Speiser: "The story commences with
one individual, and extends gradually to his family, then
to a people, and later still to a nation. Yet, it is not to be
the tale of individuals or a family or a people as such.
Rather, it is to be the story of a society in quest of an ideal.
Abraham's call, in short, marks the very beginning of the
biblical process."

Speiser goes on to comment (*Anchor Bible, Genesis, p.
88*) that "Abraham's journey to the Promised Land was
thus no routine expedition of several hundred miles. Instead, it was the start of an epic voyage in search of spiritual truth, a quest that was to constitute the central theme
of all biblical history."

What has to be emphasized here is that although this
was "a voyage in search of spiritual truth," it was never
seen (at least in Jewish tradition) as a journey only in the
spiritual sense, but rather as a very down-to-earth attach-
ment to an actual land.

God did not tell Abraham from the start which land he
was to go to. How, then, did Abraham know that he had
reached his destination?

Rabbi Levi, a third-century rabbi, gives us the answer in
Midrash Rabba (*39:10*):

"When Abraham was travelling through Aram Naha-
raim and Aram Nahor, he saw their inhabitants eating and
drinking and reveling. 'May my portion not be in this

country,' he exclaimed. But when he reached the promontory of Tyre and saw them engaged in weeding and hoeing at the proper season, he exclaimed, 'would that my portion might be in this country!' Said the Holy One, blessed be He, to him (*Genesis 12:7*): 'Unto thy seed have I given *this* land.' "

Ever since then, "this land" has remained for the people of Israel, tied with equal intensity, to both the spiritual and the earthly dimensions.

According to most Jewish authorities, the call to Abraham to go to the land is still valid today and is addressed to every Jew as a religious commandment. The Land of Israel must be faced in the "realness" of day-to-day living, and not be spiritualized into a mystical Promised Land lying somewhere beyond human reach.

Abraham had to undergo, as his descendants do today, all the *havlei klita*, the absorption pangs, of a new *oleh*. Not without justification is his *aliya* to the land considered the first of the ten trials he had to endure in order to be qualified to become the founder of the people of God. A trial it was, not only because of the hardships of the journey itself (had he travelled the same route today, he would have needed no fewer than five visas: Turkish, Syrian, Lebanese, Jordanian and Israeli, involving countless encounters with usually unfriendly and most inefficient bureaucrats), but also because of the adjustment he had to make to living conditions in the country, which were so different from those to which he was accustomed in his "old country."

Contrary to the traditional portrayal of the patriarch Abraham as a sheep-breeding nomad, recent archeological discoveries in Ur of the Chaldees, the city Abraham came from, give us a completely different picture of the country and the parental home he was commanded to leave. At the beginning of the second millennium BCE, it is now established, Ur was "a powerful, prosperous, colorful and busy capital city." It was from this center of highly developed civilization that Abraham was to cut himself off in order to establish the new model society in the Land of Promise.

If Terah, Abraham's father, who was, as we know, a manufacturer of idols, was a typical patrician homeowner in Ur, his house must have fitted the following description by a biblical archeologist:

"A large, two-story villa with 13 or 14 rooms. The lower flat was solidly built of burned brick; the upper flat, of mud brick. The walls were neatly coated with plaster and whitewashed. . . A visitor would pass through the door into a small entrance hall where there was a basin to wash the dust off hands and feet. He then continued onto the inner court, which was attractively paved, round it were grouped the reception room, the kitchen, living rooms and private rooms, and the domestic chapel. Up a stone staircase, which concealed a lavatory, the visitor would reach a gallery from which branched off the rooms belonging to members of the family and the guestrooms."

Moving from all this to a tent in Beersheba or Hebron demanded a major adjustment. It also meant abandoning the unlimited opportunities of cultural life in the big city, having to spend hours at an *ulpan*, and on top of it all becoming involved in the new, complicated religious life of the country.

Going to the Promised Land was certainly no pleasure-trip for Abraham, but we may assume that he took it in stride and did not complain too much, being aware that he had "to move away from the house of his father to the house of his father in heaven, which could be reached only in the Land of Israel." (*Midrash, Tora Shlema 12:35*).

It's the Style That Counts

ONE OF THE SECRETS of the power of the biblical narrative lies in the sharp transitions from one situation to the other, from the idyllic and tranquil to the tragic and stormy; from the personal and intimate to the universal and cosmic.

In the beginning, (*Genesis 18:1*) we are being carried over to the oak of Mamre, where we meet an idyllic scene: Abraham sitting at the entrance to his tent in the heat of the day. Looking up, he sees three men approaching and rushes to welcome them in genuine oriental style—"My lord, if I may beg you this favor, please do not go on past your servant."

The Torah reading of this week ends on quite a different note, with the tragic story of the binding of Isaac to be sacrificed on the altar. This story was always read and re-read in fear and trembling, and assumed special significance in modern Israel, which has unfortunately seen too often its beloved sons being bound for sacrifice.

We begin with a story which brings out the "human touch" in Abraham and which in Jewish tradition (but not only in it), made him into a paradigm of the virtue of *hakhnasat orhim* (extending hospitality to strangers and wayfarers).

The image of Abraham in this particular role was elaborated upon by the rabbis in Midrash who added much color and life to it. This was not only handed down from generation to generation, it was also emulated in daily life by countless Jewish families, rich and poor alike.

The Midrash asks what was Abraham doing "at the entrance to his tent in the heat of the day?" A good question. The answer: he had just undergone, as we know from the previous chapter, surgery, the operation of circumcision, and now went out for the first time to enjoy the healing energy of the ultraviolet sunrays.

A second reason for his venturing outside his tent, and even more important, was that the unusual heatwave and extra-glowing sun that prevailed on that day (God-sent to speed Abraham's recovery), kept people from taking to the road and thus left Abraham without any visitors.

This made the old man feel miserable, as he had no one to whom to extend his hospitality. When he could stand it no longer, he went outside, notwithstanding his ailment, to look for a chance passerby to bring into his home.

Abraham was sitting, we are told, at the "entrance of the tent." But what was so special about the entrance that it deserved special mention? Another good question. The answer: the entrance to the tent of Abraham that we are talking about was indeed one of four such entrances which Abraham designed for his tent, an entrance on each side, to make sure that if a stranger came from the east, he would not have to encircle the tent were the door only in the west; the same was true for strangers coming from all other sides. Abraham designed the entrances to his tent in such a way that a person should be able to get right to them no matter from which side he was arriving.

The other day, on a tour of Judea, we visited the oaks of Mamre, the place where Abraham's tent was supposed to have stood. A most remarkable thing was pointed out to us by the tour-guide: the place (near the town of Halhul on the Jerusalem-Hebron road), is situated on a high point, which actually served as a juncture for all ancient roads leading from the east (Jordan River) to the west (Mediterranean Sea) and from the north (Tyre and Mesopotamia) to the south (Egypt). Thus four entrances, from all four directions, were very appropriate for a tent standing on this spot.

How happy was Abraham when he saw the three men approaching. He did not wait for them to come to him, but rushed from the entrance of the tent to greet them. Bowing to the ground, he begged for them to visit him.

Abraham did not have the faintest idea at that moment that the strangers he hailed were important personages, angels sent from heaven. According to the Midrash, quoted in Rashi's commentary, Abraham had good reason to believe that his guests were nomadic Arabs. Nevertheless he did not receive them with cautious suspicion, but treated them with full respect and sympathy.

A hassidic story tells about a great rabbi, then poor and unknown, who often travelled to a certain city where the only person who would offer him lodging was a poor Jew who lived in the poor section of town.

As years went by and the rabbi acquired fame and fortune, he came again to visit the same city. This time the wealthy head of the community sent to welcome the rabbi, inviting him to stay in his palatial home. The rabbi gratefully accepted the invitation, but sent his horses to the house of the wealthly man, while he himself went directly to the poor home of his old host.

When the rich man came running to express his astonishment, the rabbi explained: When I used to come to this town previously, making my way by foot, you did not think of inviting me to your home. You did so now, when

I arrived in town in style, in a splendid carriage pulled by four horses. Obviously it is not me, but the horses that you pay homage to; they should therefore go to your home and be received as the "guests of honor."

Abraham had no idea that he was about to receive "important" guests. For him every person was important enough to leave whatever he was doing and run to welcome the strangers.

And what was he actually doing at that moment? Again, a good question. The answer is in the first verse of the story: "And the Lord appeared to him." Abraham was then in the midst of a meeting with God himself, who came to pay him a sick-call. Yet, as soon as he noticed the three strangers, who in his estimation were wandering Arabs, he left God waiting and ran towards them.

Hence, the Talmud (*Shabbat 127a*) derives a daring lesson: "Being hospitable to a guest ranks higher than receiving the *Shekhina* (God's presence)." God himself apparently would not mind being "put on hold" on account of a wayfaring stranger. The latter however may not be able to wait, because of hunger or thirst.

Two features stand out in Abraham's manner of entertaining his guests. First, he did everything that had to be done himself, not delegating it to his staff or aides. Secondly, all Abraham did for his guests was not done sluggishly, but in a hurry, as by one who is earnestly eager, and not merely acting in the line of duty: "And Abraham *hastened* into the tent . . . and said make ready *quickly* . . . and Abraham *ran* to the herd . . . and he *hurried* to prepare it" (*Genesis* 18:6–7).

Abraham remains to this day the great example of *Hakhnasat Orhim* (hospitality to strangers). A festive meal in a good Jewish home is not complete if there is no guest joining in the meal.

The Talmud (*Taanit 20b*) tells us that it was the custom of Rabbi Hamnuna (a third-century sage) not only on *Pessah* eve but every day of the year, whenever he would break bread, he would open widely the door of the house and declare: Whoever is in need, let him come and join.

From Abraham we learn that even when we do the right thing, it matters very much *how* we are doing it. A smile, the right gesture, the tempo in which our action is carried out, are just as important in the treatment of the stranger as is the action itself.

The Test

A RICH LIFE, packed with strife and struggle with his God and his peers is now behind him. His faithful life companion Sarah passed away upon hearing that her long-awaited only son was laid on the altar as a sacrifice. Her heart broken, she could not hold out long enough to see Isaac come down from the altar, alive and well.

Now Abraham "was old and well advanced in age." God blessed him with "everything." He was rich, respected, at peace with his God and his neighbors. One thing, however, was "eating him." Isaac, his son, was forty years old and still single, and not without problems. Isaac was an introvert, a child who grew up in the shadow of powerful parents. Now his mother had died and he had experienced the trauma of the *akeda* (the binding on the altar), which could not have left him without psychological scars.

Abraham's heart's desire was to see his son settle down, marry the right woman and continue to build the family that would become a blessing to all nations and the witness to God's presence in the world.

Abraham summons his faithful servant, "the elder of his house that ruled over all he had." (The Bible does not disclose the name of this first matchmaker, but oral tradition relates that it was Eliezer, meaning: God-my-help.) The servant is entrusted with the responsibility of going to the "old country," to Mesopotamia, to choose a wife for Isaac.

Abraham makes the servant take a solemn oath that he "shall not take a wife for my son from the daughters of the Canaanites, among whom I dwell," nor should he allow Isaac to leave the land, even if this would mean that he might stay single indefinitely.

At that crucial point in his life, Abraham's thoughts go back to his country and kindred. He realizes the dangers inherent in a "mixed marriage" should his only son choose a wife from the people among whom he lives. Knowing too well the moral standards of his neighbors, the majority population, he fears his son might assimilate, and everything—the ideals and the lifestyle which he cultivated during long years of trial and tribulation—would all but vanish.

Two ultimate concerns occupy the mind of the Patriarch Abraham as he is about to leave the land of the living: securing a burial place for his beloved wife and the fear of inter-marriage for his son. After that we hear no more of Abraham in the biblical story, but for the next 4,000 years those two concerns remain foremost in the minds of Jews in many a land. No matter how far removed a Jew may be from the ways of Jewish living, he shudders at the thought of his child "marrying out" and worries about being laid to rest among his own people. From the time of Abraham to this day, those two concerns remain the last barriers against the tides of assimilation and disintegration, which constantly threaten the descendants of Abraham.

Eliezer, the faithful servant, appreciated the seriousness of his task. He is to select the right girl to become the life mate of Isaac in building the first Jewish home, which will embody the lofty ideas fostered by the fiery, God-intoxicated trail-blazers Abraham and Sarah. How will Eliezer make sure that he makes the right choice, which will decide not only the future of the household of Abraham and Sarah, but perhaps also the future of humanity, or at least a great part of it?

The story of Eliezer's delicate mission is told at unusual length in the Bible (*Genesis 24:1-67*). What made Eliezer decide at last that Rebecca was the right girl, the one "appointed" by heaven for his master's precious son?

He did not select Rebecca because "the damsel was very fair to look upon" (*24:16*). That may have helped, but it was not the decisive factor. He did not even inquire from which school did she graduate. He certainly did not select her because of her *yichus*, the family pedigree or status in the community. Apparently he was not too favorably impressed either by her father Betuel or her brother Laban.

What was important to him was to find out whether she was kind and compassionate. He prayed: "So let it come to pass, that the damsel to whom I shall say, let down thy pitcher, I pray thee, that I may drink and she shall say, Drink and I will give thy camels drink: also, let the same be she that Thou hast appointed for Thy servant, even for Isaac."

Rebecca passed that test, and handsomely so, not only by doing what Abraham's servant expected, but also by *how* she did it. She responded with kindness and generosity, with zest and joy, and not merely as one politely doing her duty. "And she said: Drink my Lord and she *hastened* and let down her pitcher upon her hand and gave him drink. And when she had finished she said: I will draw for thy camels also, and (again) she *hastened* and emptied her pitcher into the trough and *ran again* unto the well."

This eagerness to be kind and helpful to a passing

stranger made Eliezer decide that she would be best qualified to build the first home in which the ideals and lifestyle of Abraham and Sarah will be practiced and handed
down from generation to generation.

All's Well That Ends Well

THIS TIME IT was not ideology, nor religious rivalry, nor high-sounding racial theories. The reason for their aggressive misbehavior is simple envy.

"And the man (Isaac) grew richer and richer until he was very wealthy. He acquired flocks and herds, and a large household, so that the Philistines envied him. . . And the Philistines stopped up all the wells. . . dug in the days of his father Abraham, filling them with earth" (*Genesis 26:13–15*).

On the surface they had most likely acted friendly. They must have been full of praise for the resourceful outsider who boosted the economy of the country. They must have claimed that they were unable to control those "irresponsible elements" who expressed their envy by stopping up the wells that the newcomer claimed had been dug by his father. That they were damaging the country's water supply, of vital importance to all, was less important to them than their determination to blot out all traces of this historic claim.

So, they filled the wells with earth. Not only would there be no more water, but no one was to know that there had ever been water there.

25

The Bible does not tell us how Isaac reacted to this vandalism. For all we know he kept quiet, perhaps deliberately hushing up these outbursts of bigotry. He may have been advised by his experts on "community relations" that it was better not to make an issue of the matter.

If this was indeed Isaac's calculated policy, it did not work. Following the action of the riff-raff, came the official pronouncement. It was made by none other than a good old friend. Avimelech, who only recently, when in need of Isaac's skill and capital (and perhaps his vote), had proclaimed that "anyone who molests this man and his wife shall be put to death" (*ibid. verse 11*).

Now, he played an altogether different tune. But it must be said to Avimelech's everlasting credit that he did not wrap his sinister design in diplomatic double-talk: "And Avimelech said to Isaac, Go away from us, for you have become far too big for us" (*verse 16*).

When Isaac heard the decree, he did not protest, nor put up a fight to prove his historical rights. He was certainly not happy with the decree. But he seemed to know too well that some of the alternatives open to him might be far worse. In years to come his descendants were to learn that worse than being driven out from the country which they helped build with their sweat and blood is being held captive in a land. This happened only a few generations later, in an almost identical situation in Egypt.

This was the first, but alas not the last time Isaac and his descendants were to hear the cry "Juden raus!" Raul Hilberg, in his monumental work *The Destruction of the European Jews,* sums up succinctly the three anti-Jewish policies we find enacted in history: conversion, expulsion, annihilation. "The missionaries of Christianity had said in effect: You have no right *to live among us as Jews* (solution:

conversion). The secular rulers who followed had proclaimed: You have no right *to live among us* (solution: expulsion). The German Nazis at last decreed: You have no right *to live* (solution: annihilation)."

One may find a warning of those three historical stages in the stories of the patriarchs. Abraham was subjected to religious pressure and intolerance, Isaac was expelled because of socio-economic reasons, and Jacob faced threats of annihilation from Esau as well as from Pharaoh.

"So Isaac departed from there and encamped in the wadi of Gerar" *(verse 17)*. There, out in the wilderness, he hoped to avoid the envy and enmity of the Philistines. Instead of wasting his energies in conflict and defense with hostile neighbors, he preferred independent activities.

As soon as he settled in the new territory, he went to work digging for water. As long as Isaac exerted himself in hard work, no one disturbed him. But as soon as water was found, the herdsmen of Gerar appeared, screaming "The water is ours!" *(verse 20)*.

Isaac now faced the grim reality that settling the land as he was commanded by God (26:3), was not going to be a smooth and easy task. He sized up the situation by naming the new well *Esek* (contention). He realized that there would always be contention between him and his neighbors, the herdsmen of Gerar. What he did not realize, however, until he dug a second well, was that this contention over water would develop into sheer hatred.

When Isaac's men dug another well and the Gerarians came again to dispute it, he named the second well *Sitna* (hatred). What if not hatred for the sake of hatred drove them to act this way after they had obtained, thanks to Isaac's efforts, ample water?

How did Isaac respond to this new wave of harassment? He kept to his course of bringing life and blessing to the wasteland. Reading the Bible carefully, we see that while the earlier wells were dug by the servants of Isaac, the last one he dug himself. The servants must have given up at this point, seeing that their efforts were constantly being thwarted. They must have argued with Isaac, either to leave or to take up arms against the Gerarians. Isaac was now alone in assuming a firm stand knowing that in the long run he would succeed in turning his enemies into friends. His personal example at least would convince them that they could not break him no matter how hard they tried.

As we know, this policy worked. This time, the Bible tells us, there was no quarrel over the well. So "he called the well *Rehovot,* saying, now at last, the Lord has granted us ample space to increase in the land" (*verse 22*).

The Biblical story of relations between Isaac and the Philistines does not end here. It goes on to bring us full circle, when Avimelech and his chief-of-staff come to Isaac to propose a peace treaty "now that we see plainly that the Lord has been with you" (*verse 28*).

They agree now that the facts Isaac created in the region must be reckoned with for the good of the entire region.

The story does not stop however even with the "happy end" of peace, but goes on to tell us of Isaac's continuing efforts in seeking more water sources. Isaac knew well that not one peace treaty, not even many of them, would make him fulfill God's command to "dwell in the land." This would come about only through persistent hard work of digging more and more wells of living water.

Between Two Dreams

"JACOB LEFT BEERSHEBA, and set out for Haran. He came upon a certain place and stopped there for the night, for the sun had set. Taking one of the stones of that place, he put it under his head and lay down in that place. He had a dream, a ladder was set on the ground and its top reaching to heaven, and the angels of God were ascending and descending on it" (*Genesis 28:10-12*).

Jacob did not leave his home and his country to go to Haran on a pleasure trip or to seek adventure. He was a fugitive, running for his life after being threatened by his brother Esau "who had a hatred of Jacob on account of the blessing his father had given him" (*ibid., 27:41*). Young Jacob must have been very upset, being forced to leave his idyllic life of study and personal growth in the "tents of Shem and Eber."

His mother, who warned him that Esau was scheming to murder him and advised him to flee, was now far away. He missed home and wondered what would happen now with his studies. And what about his uncle Laban, to whom he is running now, and whose reputation as a shrewd operator was not unknown even in the land of Canaan? How would he receive him? And yet, Jacob has

this marvelous dream in which heaven and earth are
joined together; he sees angels going up and down. He
receives a message of Godliness, a promise of a great future. Upon awakening he proclaims: "This is an abode of
God, a gateway to heaven!"

Notwithstanding the gloomy circumstances in which
he finds himself at that hour, Jacob is sure that God is
with him and that he will be returning home. He is a man
with a dream. A heavenly, angelic dream.

This, however, is not the only dream Jacob dreamt.
There is yet to come another dream, one quite different in
nature.

Twenty-one years elapse between the two dreams.
When the second dream comes, Jacob is settled down and
prosperous, he has two wives, children and property. He
has, in Haran, been exposed to Laban's materialistic society and values, in fact he became part of it, as he engaged
in an economic struggle with his shrewd uncle and father-
in-law to secure a livelihood for his growing family.

Jacob had just concluded a series of hard negotiations
with his senior partner, and had arrived at a seemingly
satisfactory arrangement, and, suddenly, a dream. He
tells it to his wives at a clandestine meeting in the fields:
"Once at the mating time of the flocks, I had a dream in
which I looked up and saw that the he-goats mating with
the flocks were streaked, speckled or spotted. The angel
of God said to me in the dream, 'Jacob.' I answered, 'Here
I am.' And he said, look up and see all the he-goats mating with the flock are streaked, speckled or spotted, for I
have seen all that Laban has been doing to you. I am the
God of Bethel. . . Now leave this land at once and go back
to your native land."

The dream as told by Jacob to his wives does not seem
to make sense in warranting the conclusions arrived at by

the angel of God. Now that Jacob is "making it" and even biology works for him, thanks to the ingenious invention he devised, and all the sheep "go his way," is now of all times, the time to "leave this land at once"? Why?

A closer reading will reveal to us that this last dream of Jacob did not come as suddenly as it may seem at first glance and that it is connected with Jacob's earlier dream at Bethel. There are two factors that make Jacob realize that it is high time for him to leave this land at once and return home. One is in the bad "vibes" which reach him from the sons of Laban complaining that he got rich on their back: he feels unwanted, a victim of economic envy. This Jacob should have perhaps fought and survived, but there was another factor, a more serious one, which convinced Jacob that he did not belong there, in the land of Laban and his sons.

In the language of Scripture (31:2): "And Jacob noticed that Laban's face did not appear to him as it did before" (this translation is truer to the Hebrew original than the current English translations). What was that "new face" of Laban that so startled Jacob? We know from the story told so far, that Laban's attitude toward Jacob was not particularly friendly from the beginning; what then had changed now?

May we suggest that what had startled Jacob in the "reading" of Laban's face was not that it changed from a friendly countenance to an unfriendly one, but that, on the contrary, the face of Laban appeared now to Jacob as being proper and "normal." Until now, whenever Jacob looked at Laban, and his total enslavement to materialism, he felt uneasy and it appalled him: What a strange "face!" He was constantly aware of the gap between his own values and those of Laban. Now, as he himself became immersed in the materialistic world of Laban, he suddenly realized that the face of Laban "does not appear to him [as strangely!] as it did before." Moreover, his dream has changed too. It is filled with streaked, speckled and spotted flocks instead of ascending and descending angels. "I have seen all that Laban has been doing to you," says the angel of God. The worse had happened. Laban succeeded in destroying your original dream and made you dream his material dreams. "I am the God of Bethel"—Do you still remember, Jacob, the dream you dreamt there? . . .

All that follows is a direct result of this moment of truth. At this point Jacob hears the Lord saying to him (*Genesis 31:13*): "Go back to the land of your fathers where you were born." From that moment on, he knows that he does not belong here anymore. When he summons his wives to the meeting in the field, he tells them about his upcoming plans by way of the dream he had.

Jacob finds himself again when he realizes what happened to his dream, how it changed from a dream of a ladder stretching from earth to heaven, with angels going up and down on it, to a dream of cattle, all kinds of cattle, streaked, speckled and spotted. He catches himself in time to realize that dreams filled with sheep which were, as we know, the hard currency of those days, cannot take the place of the dreams of his youthful idealism where man communicates with God. It is then, when the materialistic dreams are about to take him over, that Jacob realizes what Laban and Labanism had done to him, and that he must act now or he will not have another chance. It is then that he decides to go home, back to the land of the fathers and mothers, where he may yet recapture the old dream. Where Jacob may yet become Israel.

Planning for a Confrontation

"ONE WHO WISHES to know which tactics to use when dealing with a non-Jewish king or governor," says R. Jonathan, a third-century rabbi living in Roman-dominated Palestine, "should study closely the Torah portion dealing with the meeting of Jacob and Esau" (*Midrash Rabba 78:6*).

Indeed, the detailed preparations for this meeting, the meticulous planning of every step leading up to it and the diplomatic statements rehearsed by Jacob's messengers for every possible eventuality, provide ample material for any course in strategic planning for a risky confrontation with a potential foe.

The slightest move during a confrontation as such may lead either to lasting peace or all-out war, and must be weighed carefully.

Sometimes, the only way to achieve peace is by showing a readiness for war. But how does one ensure that even then things are kept under control?

Trying to achieve peace, one has to be especially nice on approaching the enemy and ready to make allowances of all kinds. But how does one ensure this in a way that is not interpreted as a sign of weakness which might bolster the would-be aggressor?

Many generations of Jews, who too often had to face hostile rulers, tried to look for answers to these and other questions in the story of Jacob as he moved towards the fateful meeting with his estranged brother, Esau.

Reading chapters 32–33 in Genesis, they sought to find guidance in their own predicament when faced with the Esaus of each generation. Believing in the dictum which says "the deeds of the parents are an omen for their children," and scrutinizing every word in the Bible, they nevertheless did not copy blindly, without questioning, the example set by Jacob. Often, they dared not agree with him, even criticizing openly his actions when they did not seem right according to their own temper and given historic situation.

For example, there is the comment in Midrash Rabbah (75:11): "The moment Jacob referred to Esau as 'My Lord,' said the Holy-One-Blessed-be-He: You lowered yourself eight times (*Genesis 32:5,6,19; 33:8,13,14 and 15*) to address Esau as 'My Lord,' you will be lowered therefore by the fact that there will be eight kings in Edom, prior to any king in Israel" (*see Genesis 36:31*).

The rabbis chastise Jacob not only for "buttering up" Esau by introducing himself as "your servant," and offering him lavish gifts, but also for the very fact of Jacob's seeking Esau's approval for resettling in the land which he was forced to flee earlier. While some rabbis express their opinion that Jacob needed the approval of no one to return home, others suggest that we learn from Jacob how one must live with political realities as they are. Obviously, discussing Jacob, they are debating their own existential problems during times of strife and tension between the Roman conquerers of Eretz Israel and its Jewish inhabitants.

A recorded dialogue between Rabbi Judah the Prince

(*circa 200 CE*) and his scribe Rabbi Appas gives us a sense of the mood which prevailed in those days. Rabbi Appas is requested by Rabbi Judah to compose for him a letter addressed to the Emperor Antoninus.

When Rabbi Judah sees that Rabbi Appas opened the letter with the sentence: "From Judah the Prince to Our Lord King Antoninus," he tears it up, and dictates another one: "From *your servant* Judah to Our Lord Antoninus." Rabbi Appas protested: "Why do you slight your own honour?" And Rabbi Judah replies: "Am I better than my grandfather Jacob? Did not he say (to Esau): "Thus said *your servant* Jacob."

"And Jacob sent messengers before him to Esau his brother" (32:4). Soon the messengers of peace "returned to Jacob, saying, we came to thy brother Esau, and also he cometh to meet thee, and four hundred men with him" (*verse 7*). We note a slight change in the wording of the story as related in the Bible. It makes us realize immediately that the peace delegation had failed. Jacob dispatches the messengers to "Esau, his brother," hinting that "Esau" may bring out the "brother" within him; the messengers, however, come back saying that they met not "Esau (who is) his brother" but "his brother (who is and chooses to remain so) Esau." This reversal of words also reveals what may be on the mind of the four hundred men that accompany Esau.

"Then Jacob was greatly afraid and distressed." Why this double emphasis, both "afraid" and "distressed"? The following are a few of the many explanations for Jacob's two-fold reaction of both "fear" and "distress."

"Fear" denotes, according to some commentaries, panic which is caused by something from *without*, while "distress" is caused by *inner* "angst" which overcomes a person. Jacob was "afraid" that he may be killed in the showdown with Esau; simultaneously he was "distressed" that he may kill his antagonist. Both possibilities were good cause for alarm. Something of Jacob's feelings at this point were reflected thousands of years later in the words of Golda Meir who said that "we are angry with our enemies not only for killing our sons, but also for making our sons kill."

Another explanation sees Jacob's "fear" as the *cause* for his "distress." Being promised by God himself that He will watch over him (*Genesis 28:15*) and being told explicitly (*ibid., 46:3*) "Do not fear," Jacob nevertheless could not help being afraid. At this point he realized that there is nothing to fear more than fear itself. He was distressed over the fact that he cannot overcome fear.

One more explanation is that he was "afraid" for his own life, and "distressed" over what might happen to his family. The sequence of the story tells us that of the two—the latter one was the stronger.

Every Generation—Its Dreamers

JACOB, AT LAST, after years of wanderings, hardships and conflicts, comes back to Canaan, the land of his fathers. He is now dominated by a desire to settle down and live peacefully surrounded by family, children and grandchildren.

He is well-to-do and respected. Even Esau is convinced that it is better to have Jacob as a good neighbor, than as an enemy: they work out an arrangement for co-existence in the area. Jacob's sheep are now tended by his strong, able sons, who take them far away to new pastures. The old man can now go back to enjoy his studies and muse over his youthful dreams of days gone by.

At this point, as the Midrash says, Satan appears before God and argues: "Is it not enough that the future world is set apart for the pious? What right do they have to enjoy this world too?" The trouble which comes upon Jacob at this time does not come from outside; it is not Laban who is mistreating him or the people of Shechem who are fighting him.

It is within his own house that disaster lurks. It is his own dearly beloved son, the handsome, sensitive, and precocious Joseph who is going to be the cause of strife and conflict and cause years of misery and pain to the aging father.

Later Jacob may query: "Where did I fail in the upbringing of Joseph or his brethren?" The Torah discloses at the beginning of the tale Jacob's own shortcomings in the psychology of raising children: "Now Israel loved Joseph more than all his children, because he was the son of his old age and he made him a coat of many colors" (*Genesis 37:3*).

How much was this "coat of many colors" worth? In Bible translations other than those based on the King James (which derived from the Septuagint), the original Hebrew "*ketoneth passim*" becomes "a tunic with long sleeves."

The Talmud understands it to mean a "silk shirt" and evaluates its cost at four shekels. Such a trifle token of discrimination and yet what trouble it caused. "And when his brethren saw that their father loved him more than all his brethren, they hated him and could not speak peaceably unto him."

This four-shekels worth of silk shirt was the initial cause of the exile of the children of Israel into Egypt. Four shekels thus became, as the talmudic sages emphasize, a turning point in the history of Israel.

It is truly not the amount of money involved in the wrong or right dealings with our children that counts as a major factor in shaping their future, but rather the motivation that goes with the money.

In order to introduce the elements of discrimination and jealousy among his children Jacob did not have to spend money on an expensive mink coat or a latest model racing car.

A silk shirt worth hardly four shekels was sufficient for that. Had Jacob only thought of the psychological implication of his little gift, the course of events may have turned out completely different.

That the idea suggested here is not merely a homiletic hypothesis, is proven clearly from the continuation of the story. The first thing Joseph's brothers do to give vent to their pent-up animosity towards Joseph, as he meets them in the field, is to strip the silken shirt off him (37:23).

Furthermore, they do not try to hide the violent feelings aroused within them on seeing Joseph wearing his silk shirt. When they communicate to Jacob the news of Joseph's disappearance (37:31–33), they dip the shirt in the blood of a goat which they had just killed.

Then they slash the shirt with a sword (I suggest this novel translation of *"va-ye-shalchu"* from shelah = a sword, as in Nehemiah 4:11, against the accepted "they sent," which causes problems in the syntax of the verse).

When they bring the blood-soaked shirt to Jacob they say bluntly: "This have we found. Is this *your* son's shirt?" It is hard to assume that Jacob remained oblivious to their insinuations.

At this moment he indeed recognizes the shirt and what it brought on Joseph. "Yes, this is my son's shirt," he admits ruefully and fights back: "Wild beasts have devoured *Joseph*." As if he were saying I may understand the anger caused by the silk shirt, but stripping Joseph even of his name and throwing "your son" in my face, is inhumanely cruel.

Joseph was hated by his brothers not only as a result of his father's extra love for him, but also on account of his dreams. "And Joseph dreamed a dream and he told it to his brethren and they hated him more" (37:5).

We may not be wrong in assuming that the very cause of the hatred of the brothers was the cause of Jacob's love. In Joseph, the dreamer Jacob has found a true heir and follower. He too, as we recall, was a dreamer in his youth. Every generation has its dreamers. The dreams of Jacob were very different from those of Joseph, yet they had something in common.

There is a direct continuation between the dreams of the father and the dream of the son. Jacob dreams about a ladder standing on earth and its peak reaching into heaven. Joseph supplements it with a dream of the firm earth on which this ladder is to stand.

If Jacob's ladder is to reach heaven it must be founded on firm earth, with crop-filled fields. No ladder to heaven, says Joseph's dreams, could be erected on the floating ground of wandering herdsmen. As Menachem Ussishkin, the famous Zionist leader of the past generation said: "A people has only as much heaven over its head, as it has land under its feet."

Joseph's brothers, "normal," healthy, courageous and practical shepherds were fearful of any change in their pattern of living. They could not stand therefore the dream and its dreamer.

It will take yet another several hundred years until the dream will finally come about. In the meantime, the rift between the conservative realists and the radical dreamers, between Joseph and his brothers, is inevitable.

The Return of the Assimilated Jew

"WHEN JOSEPH SAW his brothers, he recognized them; but he pretended to be a stranger, and spoke harshly to them. . . . For though Joseph recognized his brothers, they did not recognize him" (*Genesis 42:7–8*). Many of the Torah commentators were bothered with the obvious question: How come they did not recognize their brother? It's true that some years had passed since they last saw him, he was then a seventeen-year-old lad, and now he was a grown man of thirty. Yet they should have recognized him, especially since they could have had a reasonable hunch that their long-lost brother might be in Egypt.

Among the many answers to this question we find one suggesting that the brothers did not recognize Joseph, because he was beardless when they saw him last and now a beard changed his entire appearance (*Talmud*). Another explanation (*Turim*) sees the reason in the change not so much in Joseph's person as in the circumstances. The last place they could have expected to find the brother they had sold was in the court of Pharaoh, holding high office as "governor of the land."

41

Other explanations put the emphasis on the word *vayit-naker*, translated above as "he pretended to be a stranger," to suggest that he actually disguised himself, "putting his hat over his face" (*Ramban*) and deliberately changing his voice (*Rashbam*), to make sure that they did not recognize him. Indeed, the very same verb *mitnakeret* is used elsewhere in the Bible (*I Kings 14:5,6*) in the sense of dressing up to disguise, when Jeroboam's wife goes incognito to Shiloh to meet with the prophet Ahija. In other words, his brothers did not recognize Joseph due mainly to his doings.

Be that as it may, what we would like to know, even more than how come they did not recognize him, is why Joseph chose to remain a stranger to his brothers, whom he identified accurately?

To aggravate this question, let me add another, which has troubled me ever since my childhood: Jacob and his sons did not know all those years where Joseph was. All Jacob could do was to mourn the loss of his beloved son. The brothers, too, knew that they could not turn the wheel back on what they had done. Joseph, on the other hand, knew all along where his father was.

In the first years after he was sold by his brothers, he was still under the shock of what had been done to him and found himself in miserable circumstances of slavery and imprisonment which might have prevented him from contacting his folks: But why didn't he do so when he rose to power and riches?

Surely it wasn't too difficult for him to imagine the agony suffered by his father on account of his absence. Couldn't he, in all those years find an opportunity to communicate with his aged father?

The great medieval Bible commentator Ramban

(*Nahmanides*) goes to great lengths to explain Joseph's behavior as part of a premeditated scheme aimed at bringing about the gradual fulfillment of his dreams. "If we do not see it this way," says Ramban, "we would have to say that Joseph committed a grave sin in hurting his father over such a long period. . . . Even if he did not care for his brothers, he certainly should have had compassion for his aged father." Ramban is right. He should. But he did not. If we may offer a reason different from that of Nahmanides, it is that he really did not care about his folks back home. He may have wanted to cut himself off from them and preferred to forget their existence.

The trauma he experienced when his brothers sold him to the Midianites and, even more the events that followed, effected a radical change in Joseph. With the changes which took place in his career, his personality was also transformed.

Joseph the dreamer of dreams about himself and his kin turns into an interpreter of the dreams of another—those of Pharaoh. The former dreamer appears now as a most practical person, securing for himself, in a very diplomatic way, one of the top jobs in the country.

Joseph seems to like his new role as well as his "robes of fine linen" and the gold chain Pharaoh puts around his neck. It does not take long for the ex-prisoner to get used to the luxurious chariot he gets as part of his new job as second-in-command in the implementation of the New Economic Plan.

He does not want to be looked upon as a "court Jew," and does all he can to become an "insider." He welcomes the change of his name from the Hebrew Joseph to the Egyptian Zaphenath-Paneah and marries into "high society." Asenath, the daughter of Potiphera, priest of On, is probably not the daughter-in-law Jacob-Israel would have chosen if he had a say in the matter.

The handsome 30-year-old prince travels throughout

Egypt. He feels very much at home in the country. He moves in the right circles. When his first son is born, he names him Menasseh. "It is because God has made me forget all my trouble and all my father's household." The second son he names Ephraim, "because God has made me fruitful in the land of my suffering." (41:51-52).

Joseph does not think, indeed does not want to think, of the past, of the old country and the folks back home. His assimilation into Egyptian society is complete, flawless. He has no qualms about it.

This process could have gone on unobstructed. Joseph and his family might have been lost for good in Egypt, had not the appearance of his brothers suddenly thrown him back into the world he may have preferred to forget.

"And Joseph recognized his brothers . . . and recalled the dreams that he dreamed about them" (42:8-9). In an unexpected turn of events, the interpreter in the service of others was reminded that he was a dreamer himself, and his dreams concerned his own brothers. This is the precise turning point in the biblical narrative. From this moment on, the story assumes a new momentum, leading the hero from assimilation back to his own people and its dreams.

More than a thousand years later: All the oil in the Temple of Jerusalem becomes contaminated when the tide of a foreign culture (this time Hellenistic, not Egyptian) sweeps over the Jewish people. Those in high office welcome assimilation into the great culture of Hellas; their own dreams as Jews are almost forgotten. But a chain of events, starting with the act of one man in the village of Modi'in, leads to a new dedication of the Temple. This has been marked for the last 2,120 years by the festival of Hanuka, during which the story of Joseph, the first assimilated Jew to return to his people, is usually read.

Scoundrel's Haven

STAGE AFTER STAGE the drama evolves, with great suspense and mounting tension. In what is described as one of the most beautiful stories in world literature, Joseph makes himself known to his brothers.

The biblical account (*Genesis 45:1-2*) runs thus: "Joseph could no longer restrain himself in front of all the bystanders, and he called out, 'Make everyone withdraw!' And no one was present when Joseph made himself known to his brothers. And he burst out crying."

When the moment of truth came: when Joseph could no longer control his emotions and the time had come to settle his long outstanding accounts with his brothers, the order was, "Make everyone withdraw." It was one of those moments when no outsider should be present, when deep feelings should be confined to the inner circle of the close family. Only there, may one voice the grievances that demand expression. There may, indeed, be actual accusations, and old feuds may be recalled—but they should not be heard by the outside world.

Not only will an outsider not understand fully what is happening, but he may subsequently derive malicious satisfaction from it or pick on the weak points exposed during the in-fighting. Joseph understood well that no one must be present when he encountered his brothers.

A similar trait was to be demonstrated later on, in the life of another biblical figure who was destined to become the leader of his people. When the baby Moses is put into a basket of papyrus reeds and sent off to float down the river, Pharaoh's daughter finds the cradle among the reeds on the banks of the river, and on opening it "she saw the child—it was a boy—crying. She pitied him saying: It is one of the Hebrews' children" (*Exodus 2:2-6*).

If the boy she found was crying, one of the rabbis asks, why are we told that she "saw" the boy crying and not, as it should be, that she "heard" the boy crying?

Moreover, what made her decide on the spot that the foundling was one of the Hebrew's children?

The answer is that when the daughter of Pharaoh "saw" that the boy was crying with such self-control that she could not hear anything, she immediately assumed that this must be "one of the Hebrews' children." Only such a child would manage to cry inwardly, so that no one outside should hear him. A child of the Hebrews would know, as Joseph knew earlier, that he must cry among his own kin, while putting up a front as far as the outside world is concerned.

The Rabbis in the Midrash further debate Joseph's wisdom in ordering everyone to withdraw at the moment of his meeting with his brothers. Should he not have been afraid that his brothers in their rage, not knowing that he was Joseph, their lost brother, might kill him since his body guards had been withdrawn?

Says one rabbi: Joseph is to be criticized for his action.

It was unwise of him to take unnecessary risks. Another, however, says that Joseph is to be praised for his action, because of the courage he demonstrated. In his desire to save his brothers from embarrassment in front of strangers, he went as far as to jeopardize his own life. A third rabbi says Joseph was wise enough to assess the situation correctly, and to come to the conclusion that there was no real risk in doing what he did.

While it was true that his brothers did not know Joseph's real identity at that moment, he knew who they were and that they would not under any circumstances slyly kill an unguarded man. He thus relied on his brothers' basic integrity, in which he believed despite his bitter experience of their behavior to him.

Following the emotionally charged encounter, Joseph bids farewell to his brothers who are going back to Canaan to tell Jacob the good news and bring him back with them to Egypt. He cautions his brothers with one sentence: "Do not quarrel on the way." (*Genesis 45:24*).

We understand that warning, in its proper context, to mean that he was afraid that they might start reproaching each other for what had happened, and he warned them against this. But some Torah commentators see it as a warning of a different kind, with Joseph cautioning his brothers not to quarrel with *other* people they might meet on the way.

Now that they were returning to Canaan as the brothers of Joseph the powerful ruler of Egypt, he was afraid that they might feel and act superior to the people they would encounter on their way and act accordingly. He therefore found it necessary to warn them against getting themselves into trouble out of a newly-acquired, overwhelming sense of power.

The rabbis in the Talmud offer an altogether different interpretation of those parting words: "Do not quarrel on the way." They emphasize the second half of the phrase, "on the way," to mean The Way, namely Halakha or the Jewish religious way of life, and say that Joseph warned his brothers thus in order to prevent them from engaging in halakhic discussion, while *en route*.

Why such a warning at this particular moment? Perhaps Joseph feared that by using halakhic methods of argumentation, his brothers, in order to justify themselves, might arrive at the conclusion that what they had done to Joseph was actually right "according to Halakha". He wanted them to face head-on their wickedness in selling him, and draw the proper moral conclusions. Causing suffering and humiliation cannot always be condoned with the argument of "but, this is the Halakha!"

The rabbis were always aware of the danger that formal law, or speaking in the name of Halakha, might become a "haven for the scoundrel." They urge us to go beyond the letter of the law and remember that it is not a goal in itself, but rather a means to reach the higher goal of "You shall be holy."

Grandchildren and Jews

"AND JACOB LIVED in the land of Egypt seventeen years. . . and the time drew near for Israel to die" (*Genesis 47:28-29*). Within the same breath the patriarch is called both "Jacob" and "Israel." This, like other such changes in the biblical text, are not without reason.

Earlier in his career, as Jacob is about to cross over into the Promised Land, the angel of God says to him, at the end of a tough struggle: "Thy name shall be called no more Jacob, but Israel, for thou has wrestled with God and with men, and hast prevailed" (*Genesis 32:29*). This heroic period in the patriarch's life comes to an end as he is about to leave the land and go down into Egypt. "And God spoke unto *Israel* in the visions of the night, and said, *Jacob, Jacob!*" (*ibid. 46:2*). With the going down into exile, comes also a regression, from Israel back to Jacob.

Seventeen years Jacob lived in Egypt, and must have been enjoying his comfortable living conditions in the "best of the land" (*ibid. 47:6*) given to him by Pharaoh. He must have also enjoyed the company of children and grandchildren, who lived nearby; he certainly enjoyed his social status, being able to boast justly about the accomplishments of "my son the top executive of the country."

Yet, with all this, he was only Jacob. No more Israel: no more heroic wrestler with God or with men.

The approach of the end of his life shakes him out of his complacency. "And the time drew near for Israel to die," and as his mind reverts back to his own life and his own land, he is suddenly Israel again.

After 17 years as Jacob, he is again Israel, as he summons his son Joseph with his whole-hearted plea: "Bury me not, I pray thee, in Egypt."

He makes Joseph take an oath and promise to fulfill his last request. His dear son Joseph should not allow the dream of Israel to be buried in Egypt. Jacob's death should not spell the end to the fiery covenant between God and Abraham, the traumatic experience of the binding of Isaac, the wrestling with God and men of Jacob-turned-Israel. "Bury me not, I pray thee, in Egypt!"

According to the rabbis in the Midrash, Jacob did not wish to be buried, even temporarily, in Egypt, as he feared two things: that the Egyptians would accord him a royal funeral and have him buried in the tombs of the kings; and that they might convert his grave into a holy shrine. Both possibilities disturbed him equally.

Jacob was aware of how much good and glory his descendants might bring to the great Egyptian civilization. The prospect of his being buried with kings was proof of how much his family had contributed already, and might even more so in the future, to the country's political system. If this would not have been enough to convince him that their place should be in Egypt, there was the other prospect, that his grave could become a holy shrine. Just think of the valuable religious and moral contribution Jacob and his clan could make to Egyptian society!

Jacob, however, did not let himself be swayed by those temptations. He had one and only one request: "Bury me not, I pray thee, in Egypt!" He wanted to be taken home, so that his children will know where they really belong. Thus, as his days draw to the end, he wanted to be Israel again. He prefers a negligible cave in Hebron, all his own, to a glorious pyramid on the Nile built for him by others.

Joseph promises, even takes an oath, to fulfill his father's wish, "And he said, I will do, as thou hast said" (*verse 30*).

Some commentators (*Kli Yakar, Shila*) suggest an interesting twist in understanding the words of Joseph. They read them as following: "And he said, I (too, just like you) will *do* (when my time comes to die) as thou hast *said* (to ask to be buried in the land of Israel)." Which he actually did (*Genesis 50:25*).

The very last act Jacob performed was to meet his grandchildren, Ephraim and Menasseh, the children of Joseph and his Egyptian wife Asenath, who were born and raised as Egyptian princes. Upon meeting them for the last time in his life, he declares (48:5): "Thy two sons who were born unto thee in the land of Egypt before I came here are mine."

To make sure that the dream of Israel is not to be buried in Egypt, Jacob turns to the young generation. "The angel which has redeemed me from all evil, bless the lads, and let my name be named on them and the name of my fathers Abraham and Isaac" (48:15–16). Preceding this message are the words (*verse 15*) "and he blessed Joseph and said." The blessing is directed to Joseph's children, not to Joseph. It seems however that sometimes the best blessing a father could wish for himself is the blessing conferred on his children. Furthermore, Jacob is not concerned about his own children, the first generation of immigrants, who still remember the "old country" and the traditional home of Jacob in which they grew up. To make sure that the chain of tradition continues, he tries to communicate with the third generation, his grandchildren. While there are animals and birds who relate to their offspring, only humans, I believe, relate to grandchildren. For that relationship to be meaningful, one has to be able to transmit to grandchildren the tradition one received from grandparents.

Jacob knew that he was responsible for the fate of his grandchildren. If he did not transmit to them the blessings of his tradition, someone else, at a much later date, might remind them of it in most horrible ways. Thus writes philosopher Emil Fackenheim in his epoch-making work on the Holocaust: "The one million Jewish children murdered in the Nazi Holocaust died neither because of their faith, nor in spite of their faith. They were murdered because of the faith of their great-grandparents. Had these great-grandparents abandoned their Jewish faith, and failed to bring up Jewish children, then their fourth generation descendants might have been among the Nazi executioners, not among their Jewish victims."

Jacob realized that grandparents, no less than parents (who are potential grandparents) carry responsibility for the fate and faith of their grandchildren.

Who is a Jew? Not one who can boast about his Jewish grandparents (and who among us cannot boast about at least one great rabbi in the family?), but one who can speak with confidence about his Jewish grandchildren. This one can do when following in the footsteps of Jacob, who said to Joseph (48:9): "Bring them, I pray thee, unto me."

וְאַחַר בָּאוּ מֹשֶׁה וְאַהֲרֹן וַיֹּאמְרוּ
אֶל-פַּרְעֹה כֹּה-אָמַר יהוה אֱלֹהֵי
יִשְׂרָאֵל שַׁלַּח אֶת-עַמִּי

And afterwards Moses and Aaron
went in, and told Pharaoh, Thus
says the Lord God of Yisra'el,
Let my people go,

Exodus 5:1

The Beginning of the End

IN THE BEGINNING of the second book of the Torah, we are told about the enslavement and affliction of the Children of Israel in the land of Egypt. The actual event of the exodus from bondage comes much later. Yet, "Exodus" was the name given to the entire book in an early Greek translation and carried over from there to all European languages. In Jewish tradition the book is known as *Shemot*, "Names," referring to the opening verse of the book: "These are the *names*. . ." There is, however, evidence that Jews in ancient times also referred to it in Hebrew as the book of exodus from Egypt, *sefer yetziat mizrayim* (in Aramaic *mafkane*), or as *sefer ha-geulah*, the book of redemption.

Both titles of the second book of the Torah are more than just its technical designations. The fact that the Book of Redemption opens with a list of names, those of the leaders of the tribes of Israel, shows that names played an important role in the process of liberation from Egyptian slavery. What's in a name? A whole world of culture and tradition.

One of the main factors that kept the Children of Israel together as one people and merited their being liberated, was, according to early rabbinic sources (*Mekhilta, Vayikra rabba, etc.*), the fact that they did not change their original Hebrew names, trying to acculturate in Egyptian society. "They came to Egypt as Reuben, Shimon and Levi—and stayed as such."

According to biblical lore, a name represents the personality of its bearer, as well as the aspirations and directions of those who gave it. For the life of me, I do not understand why good and pious Jews in this day and age, unlike their ancestors in Egyptian bondage, reject beautiful and meaningful Hebrew names for themselves and their children. I shall never forget the shock I experienced when, on my first visit abroad, I met many learned Orthodox rabbis answering to such names as Paul and Peter.

When Jacob blessed his Egyptian-born grandchildren, saying: "Let my name be named on them, and the name of my fathers Abraham and Isaac" (*Genesis 48:16*), he expressed his wish that they be named Jacob or Israel, and not Julius or Isadore; Abraham or Isaac, not Andrew or Ignatz, or other such names, which are loaded with non-Jewish, sometimes anti-Jewish, associations.

The main theme throughout the second book of the Torah is the exodus. It comes about as a culmination of a process of liberation, which starts unrolling in the beginning of the book.

Two women, whose names appear only once in the Bible, are credited with opening the road to freedom.

"Then the king of Egypt spoke to the Hebrew midwives, one whose name was Shifrah and the other whose name was Puah. And he said: When you deliver the Hebrew women, look at the birthstool: if it is a boy kill him; if it is a girl let her live. But the midwives feared God, and did not do as the king of Egypt told them, but let the children live" (*Exodus 1:15–17*).

Here, with this heroic act of civil disobedience as two obscure working women defy the immoral orders of the mighty king, begins a process of liberation that has had resounding universal and everlasting implications. The exodus could have never taken place were it not for this first act of resistance to evil by Shifrah and Puah.

It is interesting to note that the first time the children of Israel are called *am,* "a people," is in the words of Pharaoh. The first one to become aware of their identity as a nation was not one of them, but rather their arch-enemy, the new king of Egypt, who warns his own people that "Behold *the people* of the Children of Israel are too many and too mighty" (*ibid.* 9). History has repeatedly shown that national groups do not reach self-awareness of their own strength until it is pointed out to them by their enemies, who recognize and fear it.

The king of Egypt must have realized the tremendous potential, both in terms of size and strength, of the enslaved children of Israel as a self-reliant "people" through his brief encounter with the two Hebrew midwives. How dare they disobey his orders! This certainly was not a common phenomenon in ancient Egypt: it may have been the first time that the mighty king was faced with such disobedience. It dawned on him at that moment that the strength to defy the king must represent a much larger resistance movement, which would now surely turn the masses of slaves into a unified vigorous people.

Another interpretation of the story of the two midwives throws light on an educational problem, which has been on the mind of many people in recent years. According to this interpretation, the phrase "Hebrew midwives" does not state that the midwives were themselves Hebrews, but that they were actually Egyptian women who served as midwives for the Hebrews. This view is proposed by many commentators, from Philo in the first century, through *Midrash Tadshe*, medieval Abravanel and modern exegetes like *shadal* and *malbim*. This makes their act even more heroic. We may understand how Hebrew women would muster the courage to disobey the king's orders and refuse to kill Hebrew children. But consider the significance of their deed if Shifrah and Puah were valiant Egyptian women who rebuffed the great Pharaoh. They did not say, "my country, right or wrong."

What was it that made those early "righteous gentiles," as well as those who acted in the Holocaust, different from the rest of their own people? What was it that gave them the courage to resist evil, even at the risk of their lives? The answer offered in the Bible (*verse 17*) is that the "midwives feared God and did not do as the king of Egypt commanded them."

What is this "fear of God" that gives a person the stamina of spirit to stand alone on the side of justice and morality in the face of danger? How can such a quality be instilled in the young?

Despite all the research in recent years on the phenomenon of the not-too-numerous "righteous gentiles" of the Holocaust (special mention should be made of the work in this area of Reverend Douglas K. Huneke), the answer to these questions is still not evident. The case of the Hebrew midwives is proof that dissenting individuals can resist evil, and thus start a whole process of liberation.

The Road to Freedom

THE LOWEST AND most despondent point in the story of the enslavement of the Israelites under Pharaoh is reached towards the end of the fifth chapter of Exodus. Even the contemptible collaborators, the Israelite taskmasters and foremen, complain bitterly to Pharaoh that he is asking for the impossible. How can the people produce the set quota of bricks, they ask logically, if they are not provided with the necessary raw material (*Exodus 5:16*)?

What they do not grasp is that there is no place for logic in such circumstances. Instead of a reply from their superiors, whom they serve faithfully to the hurt of their own brethren, they are brutally beaten and publicly humiliated. Violence is the brute logic at this stage of the intimidating enslavement.

"Lazy, that's what you are—lazy!. . . Now get back to work." This is all Pharaoh has to say to them. "You will not be given any straw, but you must produce your full quota of bricks" (*ibid.*, *17–18*).

Bitterness increases, but even then they do not express their resentment of Pharaoh, finding it much easier to blame Moses and Aaron. The *Kapo* never wants to hear about freedom; he would rather go on with the situation as it is, as long as his skin is saved. He does not like to think that if something drastic is not done to stop the terror, it will be his turn next.

Now he directs his anger at those who try to change things. "May the Lord look upon and punish you for making us loathsome to Pharaoh and his courtiers—putting a sword in their hand to slay us" (*ibid.*, 21). As if without the intervention of Moses and Aaron there would be no sword in the hands of Pharaoh, and life would go on peacefully. As if Jew haters, then or now, needed a special reason to provoke their hatred.

The argument, misdirected as it was, does not pass unnoticed. Moses felt hurt and lost, seeing no chance for the success of his mission. He returned to the Lord and said: "O Lord, why have you brought trouble on this people? Is this why you sent me? Ever since I went to Pharaoh to speak in your name, he has brought trouble upon this people" (*ibid.*, 22).

Thus the lowest point in the story of redemption is reached. Even Moses, the leader, is ready to give up as he sees the dismal results of his doings and hears the carpings of the people.

It is then that the Lord appears again to Moses to tell him that the road to freedom is long and full of obstacles, and that there are no short cuts. Freedom does not come easily as a result of an overnight revolt of the oppressed masses. They, the suffering masses, do not even want to recognize the fact that they are being oppressed. Redemption, God tells Moses, will come about because it is a commitment deeply rooted in the covenantal relationship with Abraham, Isaac and Jacob. Freedom will come to the "moaning Israelites" because somewhere, far away, on the horizon, a land is waiting for them, expecting them to come (6:1-5).

The message is to be transmitted by Moses to the Israelites: "Therefore say to the children of Israel, I am the Lord, and will bring you out from under the burden of the Egyptians. I will deliver you of their bondage. I will redeem you with an outstretched arm and with mighty acts of judgment. I will take you as my own people (then I will be your God)."

Redemption as it appears in this elaborate promise is not a one-time act. It evolves in no less than four stages, expressed in four different terms ("bring out," "deliver," "redeem," and "take you"). The early rabbis in the Jerusalem Talmud (*Pesahim 10:1*) cite these four uses of language as the reason for drinking four cups of wine during the Seder, when the story of the exodus is re-enacted. (Another, less homiletic, reason for the four cups of wine is that the Passover freedom meal is fashioned after the customary Greek *symposium*, which included the drinking of four cups of wine.)

A closer look at the four stages of redemption will make us wonder about the proper order of those stages. What actually comes first: being brought out from under the burden of the oppressors, or being delivered from the bondage? Does not the delivery from bondage preceed being freed from the burden? And what about the other stages: do they really follow each other consequently?

Rabbi Mordechai Hacohen, in his classic book *Al Hatora*, suggests the following sequence of events leading to the culmination of the act of redemption and the entrance to the land as the people of God, mentioned later (*ibid.*, 8).

First, "I will bring you out from under their burden." I will have your consciousness raised to realize that being in exile is an unbearable burden from which you must go out. In Hebrew the word for burden, *sivlot*, is close to the word *savlanut,* meaning patience, or *sovlanut,* meaning tolerance. Only when a people runs out of patience and feels that its condition of helplessness is intolerable is it ready for the second stage, which is the delivery from actual bondage. Mental freedom is thus a prerequisite for physical freedom.

Moreover, a freedom-loving people does not sweat and exert itself to build magnificent Pithom and Ramses for others, but dedicates its efforts to its own needs. Hence God's promise: "I will deliver you from their bondage."

That is followed by the third stage in the process of redemption. "I will redeem you with an outstretched arm." A proud, self-sufficient people stands up resolutely for its rights as an independent nation.

And only then, when they are free, self-reliant and independent, are they ready for the fourth, and final stage: "I will take you as my own people."

Trial and Error

AFTER SEVEN PLAGUES, with the eighth pending, Pharaoh yields to the pressure of his courtiers. They are careful not to allow any build-up to the image of Moses, nor show any admiration for his actions. When they appeal to Pharaoh "to do something" before it is too late and all of Egypt is destroyed, they make sure not to mention even the name of Moses.

"How long will *this one* be a snare to us?" They argue with their monarch (*Exodus 10:7*). Of course, they would not suggest that "this one," Moses be reckoned with at all as a political or military factor. He is just "a snare," but on the other hand: "Do you not realize that Egypt is ruined?"

At this point, Pharaoh summons Moses and Aaron to offer them a deal. He is ready now "in principle" to consider granting the Israelites the exit permits they requested. "You can go"—he says. "But," he inquires: "Just who will be going?" (*ibid.*, 10:8)

He is ready to let the "trouble-makers" go, but he denies there is any "Jewish problem" in Egypt. Pharaoh is insinuating that in fact only very few activists would take advantage of the historic opportunity and would actually

pack up and go. When the time comes for the actual going out of Egypt, he sneers at Moses and Aaron: "Who
will be going?"

Another interpretation suggests that the intention of
Pharaoh was to indicate to Moses the nature of the exodus
as he understood it.

"Who's who that is going?"—Ramban (*Nachmanides,*
1194–1270) interprets that since going to worship God was
a major event, Pharaoh expressed his view, that only the
important people should participate in it. Moses should
draw up a list of all the "Who's Who" among the Israelites
and make sure that the event would be attended "by invitation only," as was the style in Egypt on similar occasions.

Moses' explicit reply to both these suggestions puts
Pharaoh in his place, "We will go," Moses replies, "with
our young and old, with our sons and daughters, and
with our flocks and herds, because (the worship of) God
is for us a celebration." Sharing in the celebration of the
God of Israel is not confined to the select elite, but be-
longs to the entire people. All are included in the desire to
go out of Egypt.

"We will go with our young and with our old, with our
sons and with our daughters." Moses underscores "with
our young" first, even before the old. He wants Pharaoh
to hear about "our sons and daughters," the wonderful
spirited youth, which rose in a miraculous way during the
years of bondage.

Pharaoh's concept of a religious celebration is altogether different from that of Moses. "No," he says, "have
only the men go and worship the Lord, since that is what
you have been asking for" (*verse 11*). He is trying to im-
pose his own way of understanding on the Israelites,

whom he "graciously" lets go now to practice their religion.

"Have only the men go!" Pharaoh is the first religious male chauvinist (but not the last)! In his *macho* outlook there is no room for women, probably also not for the aged, who should stay home. But not Moses: "We will go with our young and old, with our sons and daughters." Negotiations break down. Pharaoh resumes his tough posture. Moses and Aaron, who were summoned earlier to conduct reconciliation talks are now "driven out of Pharaoh's presence" (*ibid., verse 11*).

This is not the end however. Negotiations are resumed following another two plagues, and again (10:24) Pharaoh summons Moses and Aaron and says: "Go worship the Lord. Even your children may go with you, only leave your flocks and herds behind."

And again Moses refuses flatly: "Our livestock too must go with us; not a hoof is to be left behind. We must select from it for the worship of the Lord our God as we shall not know how we are to worship the Lord until we get there" (*verse 26*).

Those last words, to all appearances uttered by Moses as a factual statement in a diplomatic exchange, express at the same time a profound theological truth. They teach us that when it comes to the worship of God, one should not expect to find ready-made formulas. True worship of God requires ever-new wonder and discovery through painful trial and error, ever-new decision and leaps of faith. "We shall not know how we are to worship the Lord, until we get there."

Rabbi Haim of Sandz, one of the great Hassidic masters who lived a hundred years ago, was wont to train his disciples in the ways of worship of the Lord.

Once, he stood at the window of the house of studies as his students were passing by: "Come here," he called over to one of them, "Tell me, if you would happen to come across a wallet full of money on the Sabbath, when a Jew is not allowed to handle money, what would you do? Would you pick it up?"

"Of course not," the young hassid rushed to answer.

"You fool, you," the master retorted, as he called over another young student: "And you, what would you do in a similar situation? Will you pick up and take the wallet full of money?"

"Oh, yes!" replied the young hassid, after hearing the reprimand the master bestowed on his friend.

"You sinner, you!" the master scolded the second hassid and called over a third one: "And what would you do?" he inquired.

The third hassid, after having listened to the master's rebuke of the two young hassidim who preceded him, replied hesitantly: "Well, I do not know. At finding the wallet full of money, I would struggle with myself in deciding whether or not to take it. I hope I would be able to make the right decision."

"At last we have the real answer," Reb Haim turned to his disciples.

Truly, "we shall not know how we are to worship the Lord until we get there."

Language of Faith

"AND WHEN ISRAEL saw the Great Hand of the Lord. . . they had faith in the Lord and in His servant Moses. . . . Then Moses and the Israelites sang this song to the Lord" (*Exodus 14:31–15:1*).

The popular saying that seeing is believing is not always true. Sometimes one may see the most wondrous things and not be moved at all. It was indeed part of the miracle which occurred at the crossing of the sea, that the Israelites looked at what they saw and were moved to faith. It was this spontaneous faith which erupted in the exalted immortal Song of the Sea.

Song and praise has remained ever since the most genuine language of faith. Most of Jewish prayer does not consist of petition and supplication, but of hymns and praises. The Song of the Sea sung by Moses and the Israelites is to this day part of the daily Jewish liturgy.

Singing to God is not without limitations, just as not singing may have fateful repercussions.

On the verse (*Exodus 14:20*): "Neither went near the other all night long," Rabbi Yohanan (*Tiberias, Galilee, third century*) comments that when the ministering angels wanted to sing hymns during the crossing of the sea, God silenced them saying: "The work of my hand is being drowned in the sea, and you chant songs?" (*TB Megilla 10b*).

This comment of Rabbi Yohanan was often quoted to show the humaneness of the Jewish attitude even towards the worst enemies. Even as the Egyptians were chasing the Israelites to push them into the sea and God wrought the miracle making the wheels of their chariots swerve, sweeping them into the water which soon covered chariot and horsemen, even then no wrathful vendetta, but consideration for the casualties of the enemy was the order of the day.

Empathy with the pained enemy was given as the reason for not reciting the full thanksgiving *hallel* prayer on Passover except for the first two days. The same sentiment was expressed in the custom of spilling out some of the wine from the cup during the *seder* night. Rabbi Yohanan's statement was hailed in many a sermon, especially by liberal and humanist rabbis. Recently however, another rabbi underscored that in fact God did not protest against Moses and the Israelites who burst into song seeing their enemies overcome by the sea. Their relief and joy was more than justified and there was no need for them to feel guilty about it. God did reprimand the ministering angels who wanted to sing hymns at that moment.

They, the angels, had not gone through the hell of suffering in Egypt. They kept up their singing even during the decades of suffering endured by the Israelites. Now that the Israelites were free and their enemies crushed, the angels wanted to join the bandwagon with the singing Israelites, whereupon God scolded them: "The work of my hand is being drowned in the sea, and you chant songs?" The song does not belong to the angels, as they had no share in the agony and suffering that preceded it.

Thus the angels were ordered to refrain from singing. We find however, another instance where it is the absence of song which is severely criticized.

This criticism comes from Bar Kapara (*Zippori, Galilee, third century*), a contemporary and compatriot of Rabbi Yohanan. God intended, says Bar Kapara, to appoint King Hezekiah as the Messiah, the ultimate redeemer of Israel. There was, however, a most serious flaw in the record of Hezekiah which prevented him from becoming the Messiah.

When Hezekiah experienced the great miracle which saved Israel from the hand of Sanherib he failed to sing praises and hymns to the Lord (*TB Sanhedrin 94a*). A person who does not know how to sing at a moment like this cannot be the Messiah!

Hezekiah was indeed a great king, one of the greatest of the Davidic dynasty. He introduced most valuable religious reforms and showed himself as an exemplary man of prayer. With all this, he also possessed an irreparable weakness; he could not sing himself or lead the people in song.

The Talmud (*ibid., 94b*) tells of the eminent achievements of Hezekiah in the field of religious education, by legislating compulsory Torah schooling. "He planted a sword at the entrance of the house of study," tells the Talmudic tradition, "and decreed that anyone who does not partake in the study of the Law shall be stabbed with a sword."

Hezekiah's biography proved that where the attraction of song and poetry of the Torah was missing, no legislation in the world, be it as coercive as it may be, would secure the dissemination of Torah and its values among the people.

Great were the number of people compelled to study

and know the Torah under the legislation of Hezekiah. The Talmud (*ibid.*) tells us of a survey that was conducted at the time which showed that there was no boy or girl, man or woman (!) from Dan to Beersheba, the northern and southern borders of the land of Israel, or from Gvat to Antipras—from east to west—who was an ignoramus, or not versed in the laws of purity and contamination.

Notwithstanding this powerful Torah network, it did not have a long-lasting effect and dissipated very soon. What is more, Hezekiah, the great Torah legislator, who alas, did not know how to sing the beauty of God and Torah, could not secure that even his own son would follow in his footsteps. King Menashe, the son of Hezekiah, is known as the most wicked among Biblical kings.

Welcoming Outside Advice

NOW JETHRO, THE priest of Midian and father-in-law of Moses, heard of everything God had done for Moses and for his people Israel, and how the Lord had brought Israel out of Egypt (*Exodus 18:1*). Hearing the news, he took off for the desert, going to meet Moses and to greet him upon his remarkable accomplishments.

True, Jethro belonged to the family. The liberator of the Israelites was his son-in-law: still, he is praised as the first outsider to react favorably to Israel's victorious march. His visit was especially important at that time as it disproved the claim of many that "the whole world is against us."

Indeed, Jethro was not the only one, not even the first one, in the outside world that heard "of all that God has done for Moses and for his people Israel." The news of the spectacular events had certainly spread far and wide and "made headlines" even further than the land of Midian. Everybody must have heard about the unusual slave revolution, leading to freedom, which had taken place in Egypt. What the Torah underlines in the case of Jethro is not only that he, the outsider, "heard" the news, but also how he interpreted it and how he reacted to it.

The rabbis in the Midrash point out that it is not only

71

what one hears that is significant, but also *how* one hears it. "One hears and gains," they say, "another hears and loses." Only a short while ago, in the Song of the Sea, we were told (*Exodus 15:4*) that the "nations heard" the same news that reached Jethro, and "they trembled . . . anguish gripped the dwellers of Philistia."

Amalek, at the outskirts of the desert, also heard—and what was their reaction? Amalek "came and attacked Israel at Rephidim" (*17:8*).

Jethro represents the exception. Not only did he rejoice with Israel during one of its best hours, but he was also, as the Talmud points out, the first to offer a formal blessing in praise of the Lord. "And Jethro said: Praised be the Lord who hath delivered you out of the hand of the Egyptians and of Pharaoh." Many pious Jews today who frequently use the phrase *baruch hashem* (Praised be the Lord) in their daily speech are probably unaware that it was the non-Jew Jethro who coined this expression.

Moses and his fold did not remain ungrateful to Jethro for the kind words he had said about them in a world filled with threatening Amaleks and nations "trembling" and "gripped with anguish" at the sight of a triumphant Israel. Jethro was feted as the guest of honor at a festive testimonial banquet given for him (*18:12*). Not an easy task for the caterers, considering the conditions in the desert and the fact that manna was the only food available.

Jethro showed his friendly attitude to Israel not only by expressing praise for what he had heard about them. As a true friend, he felt justified in offering some constructive criticism regarding the manner in which Moses conducted judicial administration.

In his over-enthusiasm for law and justice, Moses

seemed to have run himself into an administrative muddle, allowing the people to take advantage of their leader and teacher, who did not spare himself wherever and whenever they called upon him.

It was Jethro, the outsider, who realized that such a state of affairs would become unbearable. "Your are not doing right," Jethro said boldly to Moses, "you will surely wear yourself out and your people as well. This work is too heavy for you and you cannot handle it alone." (*18:18*).

Jethro not only criticized, but also offered some valuable advice for reforming the existing system. His plan called for a graded delegation of authority. He suggested to Moses that only "every major (*gadol*, large) matter" should be brought to you, while the "minor (*katan*, small) matters will be decided by them," the carefully chosen judges to be appointed by Moses. Thus, "you will make it easier for yourself and let them share the burden" (*18:22*).

The Torah tells us that Moses welcomed the suggestions made by his father-in-law. He was not afraid to admit that even he, the celebrated leader and teacher, could learn a thing or two from the world outside his own camp.

Rabbi Haim Ben Atar, the great 18th-century mystic who came from Morocco to settle in Jerusalem, where he wrote his celebrated commentary on the Torah, *Or Hahayim*, says that the very purpose of Jethro's visit to the Israelites in the wilderness was to teach us that although Torah is the all-encompassing repository of wisdom, there are things in which other people, the gentiles, excel more than the Jews. For instance, the skill of proper bureaucratic administration.

The greatness of Moses is also seen in the fact that unlike many leaders who invite expert consultants to advise them and then file away their reports, Moses immediately implemented Jethro's plan.

"Moses heeded his father-in-law and did just as he had said. Moses chose capable men out of all Israel and appointed them heads over the people—chiefs of thousands, hundreds, fifties and tens." Adding it all up we get a total of 78,600 chieftains for a population of 600,000—quite a legion of bureaucrats.

Moses introduced, however, one significant change in Jethro's plan. When reading the text carefully (*18:22 and 26*), we find that while Jethro proposed that Moses handle only major legal cases involving large sums of money (*davar gadol*), and delegate the cases dealing with smaller claims (*davar katan*) to lower courts, Moses ruled that all the hard, complex cases (*ha-davar hakashe*) be brought to him, whether they involve a hundred thousand shekels or one pruta.

Unlike Jethro, the priest of Midian, Moses was of the opinion that what matters in the pursuit of justice is not the sum involved, but rather that the proper principle be upheld.

Blind Obedience Is Not Enough

WHEN RABBI ZEIRA, a fourth-century Babylonian sage, went up to the land of Israel, he looked for a ferry to cross the river. In his burning eagerness to get to the land, he grasped a rope stretched over the river and crossed over. Thereupon, a certain gentile who was there sneered at him: "*Ama Peziza*, you hasty people that put your mouth before your ears." The gentile in this talmudic story about the love of the rabbis for Eretz Israel (*TB Ketubot 112a*) was referring, according to the Talmud, to the verse in Exodus, 24:7, where it says that the Israelites said: "All that the Lord has spoken we will do" before they said "and we will hear." Committing themselves to do, before they even had a chance to hear what was asked of them.

This declaration of the Israelites representing what a passing gentile saw as hastiness at which to sneer, was hailed by many generations of Jews as an expression of the essence of Jewish religious commitment. *Na'ase ve'nishma*, the two Hebrew words which stand for "we will do and we will hear" were considered by an ancient rabbi as a "secret of the administering angels," disclosed to Israel in a mysterious way (*TB Sabbath 88a*).

Some modern Jewish philosophers have taken those two words as evidence that the only thing that really matters in Judaism is the "doing." Judaism, they argue, is not a philosophy, but a "way of life." It requires of you first "to do" and then, if you wish, you may also "hear" what it has to say to you. The latter part, the "hearing," is unimportant, as long as one follows the earlier part, "doing."

Does full acceptance of Torah then mean that we concentrate only, or mainly, on "doing" what Torah commands? Is "Torah" to be understood as The Law, as it is wrongly translated by non-Jews following the early Greek translation of Torah into *nomus,* or shall we say that Torah means "teaching," which includes not only Law, *halakha,* to be enacted but also *aggada,* to be listened to?

Any authentic Jewish answer to these questions will have to acknowledge that Judaism means both *halakha* ("to do") and *aggada* ("to hear"). Those are regarded as two sides of the very same coin. Which then, of the two, comes first? Does the utterance of *na'ase ve'nishma,* in which "doing" precedes "hearing," necessarily represent the ideal and desirable order?

Tracing the way within scripture by which we arrive at this declaration of *na'ase ve'nishma,* we shall reveal a most startling "midrash" hidden within the text of Torah itself.

It will cast some doubts on whether such unconditional blind submission to a discipline of doing alone was really the desirable ideal of the Sinai covenant.

The story of the covenant between God and Israel at Mount Sinai, sealed by Israel's acceptance of the Torah, unfolds as a drama of many acts. "We will do and we will hear," which appears at the end of the story, is not of necessity its high point, but possibly a no-choice compromise.

At the beginning of the story we read: "And Moses went up to God" (*Exodus 19:3*). Here he is commanded, "Thus you should say to the House of Jacob and speak to the Children of Israel":

> ". . . and now if you *will hear* my voice, and keep my covenant, then you shall be my treasured possession among all the peoples" (*19:5*).

Moses as a faithful messenger fulfills the mission thrust upon him to speak to the Israelites about hearing the voice of God.

". . . and he summoned elders of the people and put before them all the words that the Lord had commanded him," namely, that the conditional prerequisite, is "if you will hear my voice." What is the response of the people to this message?

> "All the people answered as one, saying: 'All that the Lord has spoken, we will do' " (*ibid., verse 8*).

They are urged by God "to hear," but they respond, "we will do." They obviously do not want to get involved in "hearing," as they would prefer a religion that demands of them "doing"—fulfilling orders.

They argued, as later did Moses Mendelssohn of the 18th century, Yeshayahu Leibowitz of our own day (both of whom also stood alongside the souls of all Israel gathered at Sinai. . .), and Spinoza, the modern forerunner of this idea, that Judaism is but a Law, a "way of life" and not a "way of thought," of beliefs and opinions. One must remember here, that "hearing" in Hebrew does not connote only listening with your ear, but rather understanding, attaining knowledge, identifying intelligently (as in "*Sh'ma Yisrael*"—Hear O Israel (*Deuteronomy 6:4*).

Moses, the loyal messenger, does not argue with the
people. In the true style of "shuttle diplomacy," he carries
back the message of the people: "And Moses reported the
words of the people unto the Lord" (*Exodus 19:8*).

Does God accept their answer?

> "And the Lord said to Moses, "I will come to you in a
> thick cloud, in order that the people may *hear* when I
> speak with you" (*verse 9*).

Apparently, God is not ready at this stage to retreat
from his original demand that they should "hear" and not
only "do," although He moderates it somewhat. Now
they are not asked to hear God speaking directly to them,
but to listen when He is speaking to Moses.

Only following the climax of the theophany, after the
people witnessed "the thunders and lightning, the thick
cloud upon the mount and the voice of the horn exceed-
ing loud"; only after they "trembled" together with the
smoking mount that "quaked greatly"; only then, after
the Ten Words were announced, were they ready for some
kind of compromise between their readiness "to do" and
God's demand "to hear."

They then said to Moses:

"*You* speak to us, and we will *hear*. But let not God
speak to us, lest we die" (*Exodus 20:19*).

They were now ready to hear, but only what Moses
said. They were still fearful to open themselves up to the
voice of God. Thus they remain distant, choosing to be
obedient soldiers who take orders, rather than thoughtful
listeners. God, however, did not give up on His demand
that the people come close and listen.

We proceed to follow the biblical account of revelation,
detailed in a series of laws pertaining to the preservation

of life and property, as well as the observance of rituals and ceremonies. Would they realize now that they must start "hearing" in order to understand and probe the laws and their implicit intentions? Again, when the full book is presented to them, we read:

> "And all the people answered with one voice, saying: 'All the things that the Lord commanded, we will do' " (24:3).

Moses will not give up, however, until he extracts from them a commitment that includes, in addition to "doing" also "hearing." Then, at long last, they say (24:7): "All that the Lord has spoken we will do *and* we will hear."

Only at the conclusion of a long dramatic exchange do they now accept not only to act, but also to hear in the action and as a result of it, not the command by a dead letter, but the word of the living God.

Na'ase ve'nishma, two words that are pronounced now, are not necessarily two separate things following each other, as they appear in the translation "we will do *and we will* hear." They are one and the same thing. The phrase should then be rendered: "We will do *and* hear," hearing as we do, and doing as we hear. Simultaneously.

If all that God wanted was blind obedience, He would have created robots, not people in whom He implanted thinking minds and sensitive hearts.

Partnership Offer

"THE LORD SPOKE to Moses saying: Tell the Israelite people to bring Me gifts: you shall accept gifts for Me from every person whose heart so moves him" (*Exodus 25:1-2*).

He that bestowed the Law upon them; He that split the sea for their safe crossing; He that gave them the heavenly bread and provided for their upkeep in the desert—He requests now from *them*, that they shall give *Him* gifts of gold and silver and brass. Does he really need their gold or silver or brass?

No. He certainly can do without their gifts. They were not for His sake, but as a test to determine where they really stand, after unanimously proclaiming "We shall do and we shall hear."

Until they came with their gifts, it was hard, if not impossible, to fathom the extent of their real commitment. It was evidently not too hard to be swept along with the fiery excitement that engulfed everyone at the foot of Mount Sinai. Thus they called out in awe and amazement of the divine laws, "We shall do and we shall hear." Enthusiasm and vocal acceptance are much easier given than a hard penny out of one's pocket. To test the seriousness of their pledges, God ordered: "Tell the Israelite people to bring Me gifts." By your readiness to give, also by the sizes of your gifts, we shall find out if you mean what you say when you say: "We shall do and we shall hear." The question is whether you can put your pocket where your mouth is.

Besides the immediate purpose of the campaign, to collect materials for the building of a sanctuary, it also serves an educational purpose: to convert the people from passive participants in their relationship with the Lord, as constant recipients of His gifts, into active partners.

The task of bringing holiness into the world, which is the main obligation of the Jew, has always been seen in the Bible as a partnership, a combined project of humans and God. The Holy, or the Godly, can be manifested in the three dimensions of the real: in space, time and the person (depicted in an ancient Jewish mystical book as *olam*-space, *shana*-time and *nefesh*-person). God that is the sole source of the Holy, or as He is called in rabbinic language The Holy One Blessed-be-He, desires to encounter human beings by meeting them half-way as partners. In time: the Sabbath, which He sanctified (*Genesis 2:3*) and commanded them to sanctify (*Exodus 20:8*); in space: the sanctuary, about which we are told here; and in person: through the mitzva, the sacred deed, which brings us into His presence every time we perform it.

The in-dwelling of God among the people cannot take place as long as the people are passive and do nothing to help bring the sacred into the world. "And let them *make* me a sanctuary—that I may dwell among them" (*25:8*). My dwelling among them is on condition that *they* make the sanctuary. The same expression used here in the sanctification of space is used elsewhere (*Exodus 31:16*) in the sanctification of time: "And the children of Israel shall observe the Sabbath *to make* the Sabbath unto their generations." Man must start out on the path towards God, both in time and in space, in order for God to meet him half-way as his partner in the act of sanctification.

"But will God indeed dwell on the earth? Behold, the heavens and heaven of heavens cannot contain You, how much less this house that I have built!" This is the outcry of King Solomon at the dedication of the Temple in Jerusalem (*I Kings 8:27*). God, of course, is everywhere. "The whole earth is full of His glory," calls out Isaiah (*Isaiah 6:3*). And yet, both Solomon and Isaiah knew that there are special places where one goes to encounter God and be in His presence, the Sanctuary, every synagogue which was called a "minor sanctuary" (*see Ezekiel 11:16 and TB Megillah 29a*); every place set aside as sacred space for this specific purpose.

When Rabbi Naphtali of Rhopshitz, the hassidic master, was still a young child, his father chided him and said:

"Naphtali, I will give you a guilden if you tell me where is God."

"And I will give you two," the child replied on the spot, "If you tell me where He is not."

A number of things stand out in this first fund-raising campaign. First of all, that it was a truly popular campaign. There were undoubtedly a number of rich people who would have been glad to contribute by themselves all the funds required for the building of the Sanctuary. There was perhaps even one person who would have contributed the entire sum had the Sanctuary been named for

him, i.e. "The Mr. and Mrs. X Tent of Meeting." But, God
tells Moses clearly that the gifts for the building of the
sanctuary must not come from a select group of "big giv-
ers", but "from every person whose heart so moves him."
Everybody, the entire people, must participate in this
campaign.

Furthermore, it is perhaps no accident that the fund-
raising campaign (*teruma*) was announced following the
detailed set of laws (*mishpatim*) dealing with the meticulous care one must take for other people's life and property. (*Exodus 21:12–23:19*). This is to teach us that God
does not want such gifts that come from ill-gotten gain,
riches amassed from exploitation or crooked business.
Only money earned justly and honestly is qualified to
serve as a gift towards the erection of a sanctuary. This is
hinted in the words of the prophet Isaiah (56:1): "Thus
said the Lord: Keep ye justice [first] and [then] do charity."

The rabbis (*Jerusalem Talmud, Trac. Terumot*) postulated it
as law that no donation can be accepted from money that
is not earned properly. Unlike the Roman emperor who
proudly declared money to be *"non olet"* (without a bad
smell), Jewish ethics was very sensitive to the obnoxious
smell money can have, and which even offering it to the
sanctuary cannot purify.

The Caring Heart

MORE THAN FORTY verses of the Torah are devoted to elaboration of the command given to Moses to "make holy garments [or garments of holiness] for Aaron thy brother, for splendor and for beauty" (*Exodus 28:2*).

What was so important about the garments of the high priest? Does not Judaism usually concentrate on the inner quality of life, frowning on such external manifestations as clothing? What do "splendor and beauty" have in common with "garments of holiness"?

These obvious questions engaged the minds of some of the classic Torah commentators.

Some, like Nachmanides, tend to derive from here that this is precisely the lesson the Torah wants to teach us— that clothing does, or at least helps, make the person, that "splendor and beauty" are indeed an integral part of the "holy" and add much to the honor and esteem of the person who is to represent it in public office.

Just as the crown and other royal vestments command the respect of the people for their king, so do the high priest's exquisite garments enhance his position among his people.

Sefer hachinuch (14th century) goes even further to propose that the purpose of the special garments ordained for the priests was the auto-suggestive impact they would have in reminding them constantly of their role and the holiness of their calling.

However, almost all commentators agree that all the garments—and especially the detailed instructions for their production which were immortalized in the Torah— are not there merely as a manual for their makers, but are laden with mystical and symbolic meaning.

Clothing is associated in the Bible with some of the earliest signs of human civilization. Adam and Eve, when "their eyes were opened" after tasting from the forbidden fruit of knowledge, become afraid and ashamed of their nakedness (*Genesis* 2:25; 3:7,10).

The first thing God does for humans on their introduction to civilization is not to build them a home or teach them to fashion tools, but "the Lord God made for Adam and his wife coats of skin and clothed them" (*ibid.* 3:21).

God, as an active partner in early human endeavor, first appears as a tailor for both ladies and gentlemen. Some say the Hebrew word *lebush,* meaning a garment, is etymologically derived from the two words *lo bosh,* meaning no shame, as putting on clothing saved humans from shame and embarrassment over their nakedness.

In the cosmos as conceived by the Bible, and subsequently by the rabbis, clothing possesses a personality of its own and is to be regarded with respect.

Rabbi Yochanan (a leading third-century rabbi) described clothes as "dignifiers," instrumental in endowing dignity to humans.

When Rabbi Yochanan had to cross a thorn field, he would fold up his garment in order to protect it— preferring to let his legs, rather than his garment, be scratched.

Clothing was given similar respect by King David when running from the wrath of King Saul. The two met in a cave in the wilderness of Ein Gedi.

David, we are told (*I Samuel 24:5*), cut off a corner of Saul's coat to prove that he could take the life of Saul but would not.

Despite this benevolent act, he was nevertheless punished for insulting the coat of the king. And the clothes took their revenge of him years later.

As David "was old and stricken in years, they covered him with clothes, but he got no heat" (*I Kings 1:1*). The rabbis connected the two instances, and suggested that the clothes that were hurt by him, when he cut the corner of Saul's coat, refused now to give him heat, when he needed it.

Much meaning was read into every one of the garments and in making them as prescribed in the Torah. I shall deal here with only one of them, the *Ephod*, which fascinates us and catches our imagination and has generated much comment among both ancient and modern students of Torah. The description of the making of the *Ephod* and its attached *Hoshen*, or breastplate, takes up no less than thirty verses (*28:6–35*). It may be hard to get a clear picture of exactly how they were made or what they really looked like, but we do know from scripture what the main function was for this peculiar garment.

On the two stones which were part of the *Ephod* were the names of the tribes of Israel, "the names of six tribes on one stone and the names of the remaining six tribes on the other, in order of their birth" (*28:10*). The names were inscribed there so that "Aaron shall bear their names before the Lord upon his shoulders as a remembrance" (*ibid., verse 12*).

Later on we read (*verse 29*): "And Aaron shall bear the names of the children of Israel . . . upon his heart when he goes in into the holy place, for a remembrance before the Lord continually."

It seems that the design of the *Ephod* and the breast-plate is meant to teach us a most important lesson about responsible leadership. There are many leaders, who after they are elected or chosen for high office swiftly forget the people whom they are supposed to represent. The names of the twelve tribes of Israel were to be carried on the "shoulders" of Aaron, so that he should never forget the burden of their needs and always remember that he was not carried on *their* shoulders, for him to enjoy the good life of the people in high office—but that they must constantly be carried on *his* shoulders, to care for their needs and to be a loyal spokesman for them.

Furthermore, while carrying the burden of his mission on his shoulders was a must, it was not enough for a true leader of which Aaron has become an everlasting model. He must not only carry on his shoulders that which is within his line of duty, but must also fill his heart with love and compassion for each and every one of his people. Thus we are told: "And Aaron shall bear the names of the children of Israel . . . upon his heart when he goes in into the holy place for a remembrance before the Lord continually."

A great hassidic master, Rabbi Juda Zvi of Stretin, was asked how could he possibly remember and enumerate in his prayers all the names and specific requests of the hundreds of people who flocked to him with their requests for his intercession on their behalf in his prayers.

"I do not have to list them all one by one," the great Rebbe replied. "When a person comes to me and tells me of his troubles I feel so much for him and empathize with him with all my heart, until his troubles carve a scar in my heart. When my time comes to stand before God in prayer, all I have to do is to tear my heart open and cry out to our Father-in-Heaven: 'Look!' And when he looks into my heart, he can read in the scars engraved upon it every detail of the woes of all the suffering people that shared their troubles with me."

From Aaron, the first high priest of Israel we learn that a true and sincere leader carries the needs of his people on his shoulders and inscribes them on his heart.

A Political Lesson

"AND WHEN THE people saw that Moses delayed to come down from the mount, the people gathered themselves unto Aaron and said to him: 'Up, make us a god who shall go before us; as for this Moses, the man who brought us out of the land of Egypt, we know not what is become of him' " (*Exodus 32:1*).

According to the rabbis in the Midrash, Moses arrived six hours later than expected. They derive this from the usage of the word *boshesh* in the Hebrew narrative, which means delayed, but sounds like *bo shesh*, meaning came at six. Thus the Israelites did not even give themselves more than six hours to be concerned and agonize about what might have happened to their leader before they gathered to demand a replacement.

Worse than that was soon to come, when, shortly afterwards, as the Golden Calf was cast, they proclaimed: "This is your god, O Israel, which brought you out of the land of Egypt!" (*verse 4*).

This always seemed to me to be one of the most shocking passages in the Bible, while also among the most revealing as to the complexities of human nature. Moses is but a few hours late and they, without much hesitation, with little reservation, unashamedly re-write history: this calf is your god which brought you out of the land of Egypt.

Moses the prophet and architect of the exodus from Egypt; Moses the courageous spokesman and valiant fighter for their freedom; Moses the teacher and lawgiver, is all but forgotten. Now, this is their god, the Golden Calf.

How swift and how shocking! And how typical of mass psychology. They, the masses, must have a leader. What a gap between Moses and a hand-made calf! But to them this gap does not matter. "Make us a god who shall go before us!" They are ready to follow blindly any leader, be he a Moses or a Golden Calf.

One of the great rabbis of the last century who was also among the early Zionist leaders, Rabbi Shmuel Moholiver, added yet another character of mass psychology which may be learned from the story of the Golden Calf.

When Moses was late in returning and the people of Israel were in need of a leader, they turned to Aaron to make them a new leader to replace Moses. Why, asks Reb Shmuel, didn't they request of Aaron to assume leadership and step into the place of Moses? Aaron, after all, was a person they knew and loved; he was always at Moses' side from the earliest stages of the campaign for freedom.

Was he not the most "natural" successor to Moses, who had failed to return on time?

The fact that the Israelites did not appoint Aaron, but turned instead to a Golden Calf, teaches us that people seek someone from the *outside*, even if he is but a sense-less calf, rather than choose one from among themselves, with whom they are well-acquainted, even if he is as great and experienced as Aaron, their acclaimed high priest.

The same psychology, Reb Shmuel concluded, applies to many an organization and institution in our day that will seek out "guest lecturers" or "foreign experts," while overlooking and ignoring their own local talent.

On the other hand, added Reb Shmuel, we must also say a word in favor of the children of Israel in the wilderness compared to some people in our own day. They, the Israelites of old, were prepared to give up their gold to make for themselves a god. Many of us, however, are ready to give up our god, in order to make for ourselves gold.

The renowned political philosopher Michael Walzer, professor at the Institute for Advanced Study in Princeton, has recently published a new book entitled *Exodus and Revolution*, in which he draws many parallels between this and other stories in Exodus and modern liberation struggles. Moses, according to Walzer, was *the* prototypical revolutionary leader and the biblical account of the Israelites' journey to freedom is a seminal political document. It is no coincidence that the book of Exodus has been cited by St. Augustine, Thomas Aquinas, Machiavelli, John Knox, Hegel, Marx, Lincoln Steffens and liberation theologians in Latin America, among others, to support policies or score debating points.

Exodus appeals because the story is deeply embedded in western culture. The biblical account of the deliverance from Egypt is the leading model for the idea of revolution in political thought.

The crucial text in Exodus, says Walzer, is chapter 32 in which Moses calls on the Levites to use their swords against their own people, slaying about 3,000 men. Moses issues the order after coming down from Mt. Sinai with the Ten Commandments, only to find the tribes worshipping a golden calf. This longing of the Israelites to return to the habits of Egypt might be called the first counter-revolution. And the slaughter might be called the first revolutionary purge. Indeed, the episode illustrates, according to Walzer (who also wrote *Just and Unjust Wars*) a basic political problem—"when can the sword rightly be used and by whom can it rightly be used."

The account in Exodus gives itself, of course, to different readings. Alongside the Leninist reading just suggested, there is also a social democratic reading that stresses the indirection of the march and the role of Moses as a pedagogue and de-emphasizes the story of the Golden Calf. "The story could be read either way and that is why it has been read so long and so hard." However, the reading of Exodus supported by Walzer is that "the people can move only in gradual stages from bondage to freedom. . . Spiritually and politically, it is very slow, a matter of two steps forward, one step back."

A newly freed slave in 1862 America, writing to his fellows, provides a nice example. He says, "There must be no looking back to Egypt. Israel passed forty years in the Wilderness. What if we cannot see right off the green fields of Canaan? Moses could not either. We must snap the chains of Satan and educate ourselves and our children. It is a long march to freedom."

Two Sanctuaries

THE SHOCKING EVENTS would not be forgotten for a long time to come. The tensions, the turmoil, the wild orgy around the golden calf, the shattering of the tablets, the deaths and the frustration—all of these must now be pushed into the background.

The old page had to be turned over and a new one to be opened. The process of redemption that began with the exodus and continued at Sinai, must be resumed where it left off. For this purpose, Moses calls a general assembly, to include the entire community—men, women and children.

The Talmudic rabbis calculated the exact date of this unusual gathering. It was, they say, on the day after Yom Kippur, following the great reconciliation that took place on that day, as the Almighty pardoned the people for their sin of idolatry and handed over the second set of the tablets of the covenant to Moses.

No wonder Moses' face beamed following his heroic performance of dramatically and single-handedly saving his people from annihilation (*Exodus 32:15-35*). He had, also, just concluded forty days and nights without any food or drink. His unique greatness was now visible to everyone. His closeness to God put him into a class all by himself to the extent that "Aaron and all the children of Israel were afraid to come near him" (*ibid., 34:30*).

At this point, Moses could have decided to spend the rest of his life bathing in the sublime bliss of the divine, veiled and aloof from the people that had betrayed him and caused him so much trouble and pain. Instead, he loses no time after coming down from the mount and communicates with his people. It is obvious that there is something important he wishes to tell the entire congregation, the message regarding God's presence in their midst, about which he had spoken to them earlier, before the tragic events occurred (*ibid., 25:8*) when he had related to them: "And they shall make Me a sanctuary that I may dwell among them."

Rabbi Moshe ben Nahman, the famous mystic commentator known as the Ramban (1194-1270), describes this moment as the "renewal of the youthful love affair between God and His people." In the subsequent chapters, we witness the glowing spirit of dedication and generosity which overtakes the people as they become involved in the building of the tabernacle, the dwelling place for God's presence in their midst.

To make sure that this enthusiasm was not the kind which had swept them all up in its power when they collaborated to make the golden calf, Moses prefaces his words regarding the sanctuary with a reminder about the Sabbath. There are, he tells them, two sanctuaries, one in space, another one in time. The sacredness of the spatial and visible sanctuary ranks second when compared to the temporal and invisible sacredness of the Sabbath.

All work done towards building the tabernacle must cease with the onset of the Sabbath. Time was made holy by God himself (*Genesis 2:3*), while space may be sanctified by man. The holiness of the Sabbath thus surpasses the holiness of the sanctuary.

While waiting and praying for the re-building of the *beit ha-mikdash* (the Temple) for many centuries, Jews weekly entered into what A.J. Heschel called "a sanctuary in time," which moved along with them wherever they went in their wanderings. This "portable sanctuary" in time did not take the place of the other sanctuary, established in space.

On the contrary, the Sabbath in time also served as a constant reminder of their land to the people of Israel, wherever they were.

All subterranean fountains of love and longing for Zion and Jerusalem came to be openly expressed during the Sabbath. It was, so to say, an "extra-territorial" piece of longing for the firm ground of Eretz Yisrael while in the midst of shifting exiles in the Diaspora. The Sabbath liturgy and songs overflow with yearning for the return to the Land.

It is interesting to note that the Psalm customarily recited prior to grace after meals during the Sabbath is not the same one said on weekdays. All week Psalm 137 is recited: "By the rivers of Babylon there we set down and wept when we remembered Zion. . . . How can we sing the song of the Lord in a strange land?" On the Sabbath another Psalm (126) is recited: "When the Lord returned us to Zion we were like dreamers . . . Our mouths were filled with laughter and our tongues flowed with song."

Experiencing holiness in time immeasurably intensified the yearning to experience holiness in space. The Sabbath undoubtedly had much to do with the awakening of the return of Jews to their land in modern times as part of the efforts of the Zionist movement. The abnormality of life as a minority in an alien environment even under favorable conditions, was felt especially on the Sabbath, which set the Jews apart from the rest of the population which marked Sunday or Friday as their day of rest. On the Sabbath the Jew was made aware that when all is said and done, he is still considered an "outsider." There are, indeed, many "islands" in the world today where Jews can observe the Sabbath, but only in Israel is *erev shabat*, the day before the Sabbath, filled with the air of expectation, as it can be felt weekly pulsating, throbbing in anticipation, on the streets of Jerusalem.

Observing the Sabbath, with all of its restrictions, is not without problems for a nation energetically engaged in building, defending and running a modern state. It was the same for our ancestors in the desert, enthusiastically occupied with building the sanctuary, trying desperately to make up for lost time and earlier sidetracking. It is precisely because of this that Moses found it necessary to remind the Israelites about the observance of the Sabbath, prior to telling them about the building of the sanctuary.

The cessation of all work on the Sabbath occurs to make sure that even in building the sanctuary or the country, the people do not lose their sense of direction, and that the building impetus does not overwhelm them. Sabbath is the momentary pause for listening to our inner voice, a break for "station identification," lest the turmoil make us forget what we had intended to broadcast.

Open to Public Scrutiny

AS THE BUILDING of the tabernacle is completed, we are presented with a lengthy report meticulously listing every detail of the multi-faceted production. In a way it seems repetitious, but it is not so. The long list of all that went into the building of the tabernacle, which takes up several chapters of the Torah (*Exodus 35–40*), serves a very serious purpose. It comes to instruct us that accountability is a must for anyone handling public funds.

Who could be more trustworthy than Moses, about whom God Himself testifies (*Numbers 12:7*): "My servant Moses . . . is faithful in all mine house"? Who would dare suspect "irregularities" in the conduct of Moses' exemplary dedicated co-workers: master-builder Bezalel Ben Uri and gifted craftsman Ohliav—people "wise of heart" and chosen by God Himself to carry out the building of the sanctuary?

Nevertheless, "these are the accounts of the tabernacle . . . as they were rendered according to the commandment of Moses" (*Exodus 38:21*). So much gold came in from the contributions to the building campaign, so much silver, so much copper. Exact amounts and exactly where they were used in the process of the building.

The impeccable reputation of the person in charge of public funds, or the unlimited trust that he is accorded, does not suffice. Moses came to teach us that there must be an open public accounting to shut out any pretext for slander which always lies at the door of people in public office.

It is not enough that one is at peace with himself, and knows for sure that he is faultless in his dealing in public affairs. It is not enough even if God Almighty himself can bear witness to his impeccable honesty.

Claiming to have learned this lesson from Moses our teacher, the rabbis in subsequent generations ruled the Halakha (law) concerning the handling of public funds with remarkable sensitivity.

To be esteemed by people, they emphasize, is just as important as to be esteemed worthy in the eyes of God. Moses was the first to be aware of this when he imposed upon himself the act of accountability with the completion of the building of the tabernacle.

He also returned to the subject when negotiating with the tribes of Reuben, Gad and half of the tribes of Menasseh regarding their request not to cross over to the Promised Land, when he warns them (*Numbers 32:22*) to be "pure (guiltless) towards the Lord and (!) towards Israel," both the Lord and Israel on equal footing.

The same advice was also given by the wise King Solomon, when he said (*Proverbs 3:4*): "So shalt thou find favor and good understanding in the eyes of God and (!) humans."

This did not remain only in the realm of good advice, but was duly constituted as law. Here is an example from the Mishna (the earliest post-biblical Jewish code of law, edited circa 200 CE, but comprising much earlier material):

"Three times a year did they (in the Temple in Jerusa-

lem) take up money from the shekel-chamber (the trea-
sury where all the income from the annual shekel tax was
deposited), a half-month before Pessah, a half-month before Pentecost and a half-month before the Feast of
Booths. . . . He that went up to take the money from the
shekel-chamber did not wear a sleeved cloak or shoes or
sandals . . . lest if he became rich they should say that he
became rich from the money taken from the shekel-
chamber (secretly tucking away some money into his
sleeves or shoes or sandals), for a person must please humans even as he must please God." (*Trac. Shekalim 3:1-2*).

According to one Midrashic source, Moses got the idea
of issuing a financial report at this stage of his work not
only as a precaution for the future, but as a result of his
own personal experience.

Following Moses' disappointment with his people after
the incident with the Golden Calf, we are told (*Exodus
33:8*) "And it came to pass, when Moses went out unto
the Tent, that all the people rose up and stood, every man
at his tent door, and looked after Moses." Why did they
stand up "to look after Moses"? Midrash Tanhuma interprets that they were looking with "big eyes" after him, to
malign him behind his back.

"What did they say? They looked at his back and said
one to another: What a neck! What thighs! He eats that
which is ours, and drinks of that which is ours! His fellow
would reply: Fool! A man who is in charge of the tabernacle, talents of silver, talents of gold, uncounted, un-
weighed, and unnumbered—what else do you expect—
that he should not be rich?

"When Moses heard this, he said: By your lives! As
soon as the work of the tabernacle is finished, I shall render them an account. As soon as it was finished, he said
to them: These are the accounts of the tabernacle."

As long as Moses was in the midst of the work, he did

not pause to fight back his slanderers. He felt that the best and only way to fight them was to publish his records, after the project was completed.

Perhaps there is not much one can do to avoid gossip and suspicion. Yet Jewish law lays down certain rules to be followed when handling public funds.

Collecting charity for the poor must be done by at least two people jointly. It is to be distributed by a committee of three, to assure just criteria and fairness. This rule set down in the Mishna (*Trac. Peah 8:7*), is expanded in the Talmud and the various codes of law.

The collectors of charity, we are taught (*TB Baba Bathra 8b*), are not permitted to separate from one another while collecting. They must keep an eye on each other.

Furthermore, if the charity collectors have to change small coins into large ones or vice versa, they should change it with other persons, but not from their own money, lest people should say that they do not give the full value. Likewise, if they have to invest surplus funds of charity, they should invest it with others, not in any way that may seem they would derive some personal benefit from the investment (*Compare Maimonides Mishne Torah Matnot Aniyyim, 9:8-9*).

The same sources that so emphatically warn charity collectors to beware of all kinds of pitfalls that may be found on their way also have the highest praise for their work.

Says Rabbi Shmuel, the son of Isaac and Martha in the name of Rav (*ibid*): Who are those that in the language of Daniel (*12:3*) "turn many to righteousness (charity) and are likened to the stars who shine for ever and ever?" These are the collectors of charity.

LEVITICUS ויקרא

וַיִּשָּׂא אַהֲרֹן אֶת־יָדָו אֶל־הָעָם וַיְבָרְכֵם

And Aaron lifted up his hand
towards the people, and blessed
them,

Leviticus 9:22

The Significance of Sacrifice

AMBIVALENCE IN REGARD to the sacrificial cult permeates Jewish thought and literature from the time of the ancient pre-exilic prophets and the Psalms to the rabbis of the Talmud and Midrash and the major medieval philosophers, down to contemporary religious thinkers. It left its imprint on the liturgy and has been (and still is to some extent) the subject of heated debates.

It is generally thought that sacrifices of life were among the earliest and most profound expressions of the human desire to come as close as possible to God. While in English the verb "to sacrifice" means to "to make sacred," the Hebrew word for "sacrifice" (*Korban, le-hakriv*) is from the same root as "to come near, to approach."

On the one hand, the prophets Samuel (*I Samuel 15:22*), Amos (*5:21-27*), Hosea (*6:6*), Isaiah (*1:11-17*), Micha (*6:6-8*), Jeremiah (*6:20; 7:21-23*), as well as the Psalmist (*40:7; 50:12-13*), object to the performance of the sacrificial cult. With them are some of the leading rabbis in talmudic literature of the early centuries and Maimonides in his *Guide for the Perplexed* (*3:32*), and some other medieval Jewish philosophers who suggest that animal sacrifices were ordained not for their intrinsic worth, but as a means of turning the Israelites away from idol worship and human sacrifices.

On the other hand, the Torah devotes many chapters to defining the laws of sacrifices. The original Hebrew name for the third book of the Torah (called *Va-yikra* for its opening word) was *Torat Cohanim* (Priestly Code, rendered in the Septuagint as Leviticus), because a great part of it deals with the role played by the *Leviim* and *Cohanim* in the sacrificial cult. The Mishna and Talmud also devote numerous tomes to elucidating the laws of sacrifices. Maimonides himself postulates them as unquestionable law in his 14-volume *Code*.

This contradictory attitude to sacrifices becomes even more paradoxical when we face the future. Could Jews who do not wholeheartedly endorse animal sacrifice as a way of worship recite the prayers for the full restoration of sacrifices, which occupy a central place in the traditional Jewish prayer book?

Sacrifices do indeed present an esthetic, sometimes a moral, problem to many modern Jews who are unable to envision being spiritually uplifted at the sight of slaughtered animals, spilled blood and burning incense. Yet, with all the reservations prophets, rabbis and philosophers have expressed about sacrifices they are indisputably an integral part of Torah legislation, as well as of Jewish history in the First and Second Temples. They are also included in the aspirations concerning the third temple, for whose speedy rebuilding Jews pray daily according to the traditional prayer book.

Some leading modern Jewish thinkers (i.e., Harav Kook, Franz Rosenzweig) have argued that we should not press the issue in trying to decipher the mystery of sacrifices until it presents itself again as part of a new eschatological reality which may well alter some prevailing sensitivities or reveal new insights into old ones.

What is left then for us to do in dealing with the chapters of the sacrifices in the Torah is to learn from them, each one according to his own understanding, a lesson for today. Many indeed are the lessons one can learn while reading the first chapters of Leviticus which lead us to the chapters dealing with our ability and obligation to live a life of holiness.

Although dealing with a Priestly Code, the Torah does not turn first to the Levites and priests, but to the entire people.

"Speak to the children of Israel, and say unto them, if any man of you bring an offering unto the Lord, ye shall bring your offering of the cattle, even of the herd, and of the flock" (*Leviticus 1:2*). Thus the translation of the Authorized Version, followed with minor changes in other English translations. When one goes back however, to the original Hebrew, one finds the order of the verse puzzling, as it reads in the following manner: ". . . and say unto them, if any person bring *of yourselves* a sacrifice unto the Lord, etc." Not "any man (or person) of you," but "bring of you (or of yourselves) an offering (or sacrifice)." This somewhat awkward turn of phrase gave room to a number of interpretations, all sharing the common denominater that the Torah demands here that the sacrifice must be part of *yourselves*. God does not want a sacrifice which does not rightfully belong to you personally, or which you do not see as if you yourselves were vicariously offered on the altar.

When by the grace of God, one is allowed to substitute the sacrifice of an animal for the sacrifice of one's self (as happened to Isaac, who remained the prototype of all offerings), one should bring it "from the herd and the flock." Furthermore, when making an offering one must not bring something that does not really belong to him, not wild hunt, nor "surplus" materials, but a bull or a

goat that comes from one's own flock. A person's riches
were measured in ancient times by the size of his herd.
Sheep and cattle were what money is to us. When one
makes an offering, one must teach himself to give away
that which he needs for himself, not only that which is
surplus, or can be taken off as an income tax deduction.

When we were children, we were told the following
story: A wealthy man died and bequeathed his three sons
three precious gifts. The first son received a pair of binoculars through which he could see from one end of the
world to the other. The second son received a magic carpet, which could carry its passengers to the end of the
world in one instant, and the third son received an apple
that upon eating it one could utter any wish and it would
be fulfilled.

One day the son with the binoculars looked and saw
that somewhere in a far-away country, a beautiful princess, the only daughter of a great king was dreadfully
sick. As no doctor could cure her, the king declared that
any person who would restore the health of his dearly
beloved daughter would be given her hand in marriage
and eventually become king. Upon seeing this, he summoned his brothers and the three of them mounted the
magic carpet, arriving in an instant in that far-away land.
The princess ate the enchanted apple, made her wish to
recover and was instantly healed.

Now each one of the three sons came to the king,
claiming that he deserved to marry the king's daughter.
Said the first one: "If it were not for my binoculars we
would have never known of the princess's illness and
would not have come to heal her. I therefore am the one
who deserves to marry the princess."

Said the second one: "If it were not for my magic carpet, we could have never arrived here in time to save the life of the princess. The binoculars and apple would not have been any good without my carpet!"

Said the third son: "Neither the binoculars nor the carpet would have been any good, were it not for my apple that actually was used to cure her."

The king, of course, saw the point made by every one of the three sons as each one gave a convincing argument, showing he should be the one chosen. He had to decide, however which of the three would be the one to marry his only daughter. What was his decision? And why?

As children we were asked how to solve the king's dilemma and make the right decision. It is a difficult one.

A clue to the right answer is to be found in the portion of the Torah dealing with the sacrifices.

Balancing Fire and Light

"THE LORD SPOKE to Moses, saying: 'Command
Aaron and his sons thus: This is the ritual of the burnt
offering . . . it shall remain where it is burned upon the
altar until morning, while the fire on the altar is kept going on it' " (*Leviticus* 6:1,2). Again, three verses later:
"The fire on the altar shall be kept burning, not to go out."
And again, the next verse: "A perpetual fire shall be kept
burning on the altar, not to go out."

The above quotes are taken from the new Jewish Publication Society translation. Most of the other English translations of the Bible we consulted offer similar translations,
with the exception of the Authorized King James version,
which in this case is truer to the Hebrew original in that it
distinguishes clearly between the fire burning *on* the altar
(*al* ha-mizbeach) and the fire burning *in* it (tukad *bo*), or, if
you wish, *in* him, namely in the officiating priest.

It is not enough to have a fire burning on the altar, says
the hassidic interpretation pointedly, emphasizing that
there must also be "a perpetual fire" of enthusiasm
within us when we truly worship God.

"The inflaming," the ardour of ecstasy, known in hassidic thought as *hitlahavut*, says Martin Buber (in his *Hasidism and Modern Man*) "is the goblet of grace and the eternal key."

Elie Wiesel tells of the poet who was asked, "If you could save from your burning home only one thing, what would that be?" "The fire," the poet answered, for without it life would not be worth living.

The introduction of fire marks the beginnings of civilization. Primitive man worshipped fire. It provided warmth, food, light, tools and weapons; it enabled him to shape the world around him. Man came to regard fire as an all powerful god, as do some people to this day, except that the fire-worshippers of today use a more sophisticated nomenclature, calling it energy or technology.

Torah and Jewish tradition also play much with fire. God's word comes to us in flames of fire (*Exodus 3:2;19:18; Jeremiah 23:29*). A "perpetual fire" must burn on the altar (*Leviticus 6:16*), and in many similar instances in the Bible the importance of fire is stressed. The Bible makes us realize, however, that while God may speak out of fire, fire is not God. While fire shapes things, it does not create them. God wants man to use fire and technology, not to be dominated and subordinated by them.

The world comes into being, according to the biblical story, with God solemnly pronouncing: "Let there be light." This first act of the creation of "light" includes most likely also the creation of all sources of energy. The creation of fire as such is not mentioned explicitly in the story. Rabbinic tradition fills in the missing gap.

Crowning the end of the biblical story of creation is the creation of Adam and Eve. Soon after their coming into the world comes the first Sabbath. When the first Sabbath was over, Adam saw the sun go down for the first time and an ever-deepening gloom enfold the created world. Adam's heart was filled with terror; he felt helplessly lost in the dark. God then took pity on him and endowed him with the intuition to take two stones and rub them against each other, and so to discover fire, whereupon he gratefully exclaimed: "Blessed be the creator of the lights of fire."

This story stands in direct contrast to Greek mythology, which represents Prometheus as *stealing* fire from the jealous gods and secretly giving it to humans, for which he is chained to a rock and tortured endlessly. In Jewish tradition fire is not stolen, nor held back from humans; it is a heavenly gift to man to enable him to become partner with God in continuing to create the world and improve it.

The biblical story of creation is re-enacted every Sabbath in Jewish homes. The Sabbath is ushered in with a blessing over the lights, just as God in the beginning pronounced: "Let there be light." After six fiery days of creative work, God teaches man that a moment comes when all labor, even that of creation, must cease in order to make room for the life of the soul. Man must remember that after the six days that were given to us "to do," we were given one more day "to be." Six days a week we are identified by what we *do*; one day by who we *are*.

The parting of the Sabbath takes place with the Havdala ceremony, which includes lighting a torch of fire and pronouncing a blessing to the "Creator of the Lights of Fire." Sabbath enters with light and departs with fire.

Sabbath itself was called a day of "joy and light." Fire must not be kindled on the Sabbath "in all your dwellings" (*Exodus 35:3*). The one exception is the perpetual fire on the altar, which must be kept aflame even on the Sabbath (*TJ Yoma* 6:4). It is in the sanctuary where both the "eternal light" (*Exodus* 27:20) and the "eternal fire" are kept.

Both light and fire are gifts of God and we need both of them. The right balance between the light of grace (*hesed*) and the fire of power (*gebura*), between the fire of creativity and the light of the awareness that we are ourselves created and kept alive by God, is the secret of the good life in the eyes of the Torah. The positive precepts, all the "do's," were likened to light; the negative, all the "don't's,"—to fire. Both together make one complete Torah.

Fire and its more modern transfiguration, technology, are there to serve humanity, not to enslave it. Misuse of fire is likely to destroy and bring the world back to Chaos and *tohu*; the right use of fire which is perpetually kept in the sanctuary can bring blessing, warmth and light.

Why Kashrut?

IN THE FOURTH century B.C.E., Cleachus, a pupil of Aristotle, reported that his master had a discourse with a Jew and came away from it deeply impressed with two things about the Jews: their admirable philosophy and their strict diet.

Today, 2,500 years after Aristotle, everybody knows about the Jewish diet, known as kosher food. One has had no problem at all ordering a kosher meal on a Chinese Airlines flight from Peking to Tokyo. The word "kosher" has entered into every English language dictionary. And yet, we know so little about *kashrut*, why some foods may be eaten and others not. What makes some beasts and birds "clean," or kosher, others "not clean," *taref*?

Probably no other subject in the Torah has elicited so many explanations and speculative justifications as the dietary restrictions. From Philo, in first-century Alexandria, down to contemporary anthropologists and religious apologetics, we find ever new theories attempting to grasp the meaning behind the long catalogues of permitted and prohibited foods which take up so much space in Torah and are central to Jewish life throughout the ages.

Firstly, there are the forbidden insects, fish, fowl and

animals. The dietary laws also require that the animal be slaughtered in a certain way and its blood drained in a specific manner. Another requirement is that meat and dairy foods must neither be eaten nor cooked together.

Torah itself gives no reason for the restrictions, except for the prohibition of blood: "Since the life of a living body is in its blood" (*Leviticus 17:11-12*). As to all other dietary laws, there is an overall stated purpose: ". . . For I am the Lord who brought you out from the land of Egypt to be your God; ye shall therefore be holy, because I am holy." (*Leviticus 11:45-47*).

From the above, as from the other texts where Torah tells us of the various aspects of kashrut (*see Exodus 22:30; Deuteronomy 14:21*), it is clear that the purpose of kashrut is holiness. This does away with the argument voiced by many a modern Jew: "It may have had its place in antiquity, but with modern methods of slaughtering, regular government inspection and sanitary food preparation, kashrut is an anachronism which should be discarded along with the horse and carriage."

Maimonides' idea that the motive behind kashrut is to achieve good health was already repudiated hundreds of years ago. Among others, Rabbi Isaac Arama (1420-94) in his *Akedat Yitzhak*, disputes Maimonides' views on this subject: "The dietary laws are not, as some have suggested, motivated by therapeutic considerations, God forbid! Were that so, the Torah would be denigrated to the status of a minor medical treatise and worse."

The idea that "nurture shapes nature," or as the Germans put it, *"Der Mensch ist was er esst,"* goes as far back as Philo, who wrote 2,000 years ago that the eating of the prescribed kosher food is bound to affect our personalities. The dietary laws, he explains, are intended to teach us to control our bodily appetites. While Moses did not demand Spartan self-denial, he forbade pork, the most delicious of all meats, in order to discourage excessive self-indulgence. He further prohibited the eating of carnivorous beasts and birds, in order to teach us gentleness and kindness. Philo finds a symbolic meaning in the permission to eat of animals that chew their cud and have divided hoofs; man grows in wisdom only if he repeats and chews over what he has studied and as he learns to divide and distinguish various concepts (Philo, *The Special Laws IV, 97f.*)

One of the pragmatic explanations for the dietary laws has it that they were ordained in order to separate the Jews from their gentile environment. Whether this was intended or not, phenomenologically the laws of kashrut did indeed serve as a powerful social factor in guarding Jewish survival against assimilation. To this day, it provides an effective meeting ground for Jews, at home or when travelling on the road. Kosher restaurants everywhere are a place where one Jew meets another to find some familiarity and warmth in this big and alien world.

Another school of interpretation of kashrut is the symbolic, spanning from Philo to modern times. Outstanding voices in this school, in addition to the Orthodox apologetics (like Sampson Rafael Hirsch, Dayan Grunfeld and others), are those of British anthropologist Mary Douglas and French structuralist Jean Soler. The underlying perception shared by the last two is that the dietary prohibitions are a kind of symbolic language to transmit a sense of reality reflecting the concept of the holiness of God which Israel is required to share.

The overriding rationale which emerges from all the various insights into the meaning of the dietary laws is that Torah legislates to invoke in us reverence for life. To some, this is the essential moral lesson of kashrut. Dennis Prager and Joseph Telushkin, in their popular book *Nine*

Questions People Ask About Judaism, would go even a step further, saying that "keeping kosher is Judaism's compromise with its ideal of obtaining food without killing, namely, vegetarianism."

Ideally, according to Torah, humans would confine their eating to fruits and vegetables and not kill for food. In the Garden of Eden, man was originally commanded to be vegetarian (*Genesis 1:28–29*). The future eschatological utopia is also depicted as one in which all creatures will be vegetarian (*Isaiah 11:7*). The Torah refers negatively to meat-eating as to an uncontrollable "craving." Realizing that it would be hard if not impossible to curb humans from their "craving" for meat, Torah does not ordain absolute vegetarianism, which would be the ideal, but instead ordains kashrut.

Accordingly, the laws of kashrut come to teach us that a Jew's first preference should be a vegetarian meal. If however one cannot control a craving for meat, it should be kosher meat, which would serve as a reminder that the animal being eaten is a creature of God, that the death of such a creature cannot be taken lightly, that hunting for sport is forbidden, that we cannot treat any living thing callously, and that we are responsible for what happens to other beings (human or animal) even if we did not personally come into contact with them.

As an example of the latter concern, we are told of a Boston rabbinical court that some years ago declared grapes picked by oppressed Chicano workers to be non-kosher. This suggests that perhaps one may similarly declare the skins of baby seals that were clubbed to death non-kosher to wear.

Kosher does not mean "clean" nor "holy" or "blessed" by a Rabbi. Kosher means proper. The purpose of the laws of kashrut is to help us choose guidelines to what is proper in our habits in this basic human activity of eating, and our treatment of living things in general.

In his last speech at the Zionist Congress in Jerusalem in 1972, Abraham Joshua Heschel lauded the fact that most hotels in Israel are *kosher*. He added that this is not enough. As we have *mashgichim* supervising the *kashrut* in restaurants and butcher shops, we should also put them in banks and factories. A drop of blood in an egg makes it non-kosher, how about spots of blood, Heschel asked, in a dollar or sheckel?

The Mystery of Birth

ONE NEED NOT travel far to be able to observe the most wondrous spectacle on earth. It is right here beside us: a human being. Jewish daily prayer which calls for radical amazement at God's world, begins with pronouncements over the human body (*asher yatzar*) and soul (*elohai neshama*).

The study of biology and genetics has made tremendous strides in recent decades. We are able, as never before, to manipulate many of the functions of our bodies. Transplants of vital organs have become an everyday occurrence. Notwithstanding all of this, we are just as puzzled and fascinated by the birth of a single baby as our ancestors were, thousands of years ago. Who can explain how a drop of seed travels to unite with an ovulated egg and becomes a person, endowed with a divine image, by the spiritual essence contained within the material? This process, it seems, was and still remains an unfathomable mystery.

There is hardly any information offered in the Bible about conception and birth. Sure enough, psalmists and prophets praise the maker of this astonishing complex creature, but they tell us little to help us comprehend it.

There seems to be a deliberate tendency towards de-mythologization of the subject in biblical sources. The birth of the first human children could not have been announced in a more formal and factual way. "Now Adam had known his wife Eve and she conceived" (*Genesis 4:1*).

The verb *yda*, "to know" personally and intimately, is the usual biblical term for the sexual act. It has no mythical connotations whatsoever, no gods or goddesses are involved, not even storks or eagles. It is a direct but subtle linguistic expression for an act which the Bible sees as private, delicate and modest.

Biblical writers were not, as a rule, overly prudish in matters of sex. Had they wished, they could have put it the way this verse is rendered in the New English Bible (Oxford University Press, Cambridge University Press): "The man lay with his wife Eve." Not having been educated in Oxbridge, however, they tried to choose a verb which reflected a certain more refined attitude toward sexuality.

Sensitivity to language aside, Torah does not treat the subject romantically, nor does it wrap it in a mysterious aura, but, rather, it is direct and factual. "When a woman conceives and bears a male child, she shall be unclean for seven days, as in the period of her impurity through menstruation" (*Leviticus 12:2*). Pregnancy and birth are dealt with in a matter-of-fact manner, yet this does not dispel the mystery surrounding them.

Why the impurity caused by birth? Why is the new mother obliged to bring a sin offering? Isn't birth the fulfillment of a positive commandment given to mankind to "be fruitful and multiply" (*Genesis 1:28*)? And what of impurity imposed on women during menstruation?

To quote the Encyclopedia Judaica (in the article *Nid-*

dah): "The laws relating to the menstruous woman comprise some of the most fundamental principles of the halakhic [Jewish Religious Law] system, while a scrupulous observance of their minutia has been one of the distinguishing signs of an exemplary traditional Jewish family life." Few will contradict this, nor the statement which follows it, claiming that those laws are "among the most difficult and intricate in the entire range of the halakha."

In talmudic and midrashic literature, there is much praise accorded to Jewish women and men who adhere to the strict laws of purity and impurity in sexual relations. The laws of *niddah* are among the few laws of impurity left of a huge complex legislature in this area during Temple times. We find, however, very few attempts to rationalize the laws. Also medieval Jewish philosophy had little to say on the subject.

It is only in modern times that a vast literature grew to offer various "reasons" for those laws, which of late were also given the more palatable appellation *taharat hamishpaha*, or "family purity." Those rationales range from the medical to the psychological, the philosophical and the sociological and even the cosmic (see Rabbi Norman Lamm's *Hedge of Roses* and many other publications on the subject proliferating in recent years). The sum total of all those explanations drives us, however, to the conclusion that rationality does not suffice, unless one considers the laws of *niddah* as part of the mystery surrounding pregnancy and birth, still far from being deciphered.

In their attempt to penetrate the mystery, the talmudic rabbis ask: What happens to the "person" prior to his or her appearance in this world? Rabbi Simlai, a third-century rabbi, relates the following (*TB Niddah 30*): "The fetus when in its mother's womb, is folded like a notebook, its head rests on its two temples, its two elbows on its two legs and its two heels against its buttocks. Its head lies between its knees, its mouth is closed and its navel is open, and it eats what its mother eats and drinks what its mother drinks . . . A light burns above its head and it looks and sees from one end of the world to the other . . . There is no time in which a person enjoys greater happiness than in those days . . . it learns the entire Torah and as it is about to be born, an angel approaches, slaps it on its mouth and causes it to forget all the Torah." Folklore has it that the indentation of the upper lip is a result of that angelic touch.

The talmudic description should not be taken only as fanciful folklore. Without Freudian teachings or ultrasound screening, it comes to convey to us certain ideas on the pre-natal existence of humankind. The seeing "from one end of the world to the other" is explained in the Talmud as the source of human imagination that takes us to the ends of the world often accompanied with a sense of *déjà vu*. The learning of Torah at this early stage conveys a Platonic idea that education is primarily a process of reminiscing about things we knew previously.

The same source, where the formation of the embryo in its various stages is discussed, states also that "there are three partners in Man: God, father, and mother. The father supplies the white substance of which the child's bones, sinews, nails, brain and the white of the eyes are formed. The mother supplies the red substance of which are formed skin, flesh, hair, blood, and the dark of the eyes. God supplies the spirit, the breath, beauty of features, eyesight, hearing and the ability to speak and to walk, understanding and discernment . . ."

I do not know whether the biological theory offered here is valid scientifically, but the intention of this rabbinic homily is obvious. It aims to drive home the idea that the human genes produce only the material composition of the body, while seeing, hearing, spirit and intellect are God-given. It says that the human comes to this world not only as a physical being, but also as one bearing the divine image and the freedom that comes with it. Furthermore, his humanity is not something which can be taken or rejected at will. "As the child is about to emerge into this world," the rabbis continue, "he must take an oath, that he will be righteous and not wicked and never follow mass public opinion in this matter."

The human is born in his aloneness with the capacity to choose between good and evil. He is not, as Heidegger would have it, "thrown into the world," but put there for a specific purpose. He has indeed learned Torah before birth, but learning can come and go with the snap of a finger. Goodness is not inherited, but must be acquired in a lifetime of decision-making. Every day, every moment, a person must decide between good and evil.

Torah too, is not given. One must acquire it in great effort. "If the fetus learns all of Torah while in its mother's womb," asks a hassidic master, "why make it forget all that it learned? And conversely, if he forgets it anyway, why invest efforts in teaching it to him? What is the good of Torah in the mother's womb?"

He asked the question and answered it with a parable: Once a great king traveled through a forest when he suddenly heard the sound of beautiful music. He became enthralled with the melody and rushed in the direction where the music came from; as he got there, it seemed to him that the music came from the opposite direction. When he ran there, it again appeared to be coming from still another direction.

He spent the day running in all directions, enchanted by the beautiful melody, but could not find the musicians nor catch the melody. After much running about and searching, he returned to his palace, but the melody he heard in the forest was still haunting him. He summoned all the bands and musicians in the land to his court and asked them to play for him their entire repertoire with the hope that they would come to the melody he lost in the forest, but to no avail. They played many beautiful enchanting melodies, but not the one he was looking for. Sometimes, they even came close to playing it, but never hit the right chord. The king thus learned many melodies, but he also knew that he had to keep up the search for "the" melody.

Likewise, we are made to forget the Torah we studied while still in our mother's womb. But, what it does to us is give us the feeling that with all the Torah we study, we must keep on looking for the "real" Torah, which we learned from the divine angel before we came to this world.

Though we have forgotten it, enough has remained with us for us to know, always, that there is still more of Torah we have yet to learn.

The Lethal Tongue

THE TIME: EARLY third century, around the year 220. The place: the bustling town of Sepphoris in Upper Galilee. The great Rabbi Yannai is in his study, expounding the Scriptures.

The loud voice of a street peddler is heard, chanting: "Who wishes to purchase the elixir of life, the elixir of life?" Rabbi Yannai looks out of his window, sees crowds around the peddler and summons him to come up and sell him some of the magic elixir. The peddler answers: "What I am selling is not for you, rabbi."

When the rabbi insists, the peddler takes the book of Psalms and points to the passage that says: "Who is the person that desires life?" And to what follows: "Keep your tongue from evil."

Rabbi Yannai, continues the Midrash (*Vayikra Rabba 16*, where the above story is told), then said: All my life I have been reading this passage, but did not know how to explain it, until this hawker came and made it clear to me. Now I see how the very same idea is expressed by King Solomon, who proclaims (*Proverbs 21:23*): "He who guards his mouth and tongue guards his soul from trouble."

When we realize the historical setting of this story, we may assume that it is not as innocent as it may seem on the surface. The land of Israel, in particular the Galilee, was at that time in turmoil, with revolts and insurrections in defiance of the Roman conquerers. The Roman legionnaires and their spies and informers were roaming the country constantly on the search for rebels and freedom fighters.

The peddler must have surreptitiously been passing the word among the people of Sepphoris, that they should beware of speaking about certain persons or things that might lead to interrogation.

Rabbi Yannai, by adding his own remarks to those of the peddler, made it known that he too supported the clandestine message transmitted on to the people of Sepphoris—i.e., you who desire life, guard your tongues!

The context in which the story is told is the exposition of the laws of leprosy in the Torah (*Leviticus 14:1–15:33*). Very seldom does Jewish thought suggest a direct link between a certain transgression and its specific divine punishment. Leprosy is the rare exception, being closely linked with the sin that caused it, namely, *Lashon ha-ra*, a term which covers slander, gossip, tale-bearing and all the other forms of damage to the individual and society that may be caused by words.

Miriam, (*Numbers 12:1–16*), speaks against Moses behind his back and is swiftly visited with leprosy. This is one of many instances cited by the rabbis to prove the direct connection between the person who opens his mouth secretly, whispering his stories, assuming that no one will discover the source of the gossip, and his justly deserved punishment: leprosy, an illness which cannot be hidden.

"This is the law of the *metzora* (leper)" became the staple text for countless rabbinic homilies against the spread of *lashon ha-ra*. *Metzora*, they repeated over and over again, sounds just like *motzi-ra*, i.e., one who utters evil with his mouth. The crime and its punishment in one word.

Jewish tradition sees a lethal weapon in the evil tongue and minces no words in its condemnation. The Talmud equates speaking *lashon ha-ra* with flagrant atheism, with adultery and with murder. In fact, it is worse than murder, since it simultaneously destroys three people—the one who relates the gossip, the one who listens to it, and the one it concerns.

The prophet Jeremiah (9:7) is quoted: "their tongue is a deadly arrow, it speaks deceit. One speaks peacefully to his neighbor with his mouth, but in his heart he layeth wait for him." Murdering with an arrow is sly, it is uglier than murdering with a sword. *L'shon ha-ra* is like murder with an arrow, where perpetrator and victim do not face each other. One who assassinates the character of his fellow by spreading around gossip is not only a cold-blooded murderer, he is also a loathsome coward.

Strong as their condemnation of *lashon ha-ra* was, the rabbis of the Talmud recognized how hard it is to prevent it. "There is hardly a day when we are spared from it," they admit (*Baba Bathra 164b*). They were aware of and cautioned us against the many rationalizations with which people condone the uttering of derogatory statements, offering such excuses as "But I was only joking," "This won't hurt him," or "Everybody knows it anyway."

Every Jewish moralist writer cries out against the pitfalls of *lashon ha-ra*. Every legal code emphasizes its severity. There was, however, one great rabbi in recent times who made it his life's goal to teach people of the dangers of *lashon ha-ra* and how to keep away from it.

His name was Rabbi Israel Meir Hacohen Kagan (1839–1934), but he is known throughout the Jewish world by the name of his book, *Hafetz Hayim*; by that name he is also commemorated in a religious kibbutz in the south of Israel, Kibbutz Hafetz Hayim. The rabbi took the name of his book from the verse in Psalms (34:13–14): "Whoso is the man that desires life (*mi ha-ish he-hafetz hayim*)—keep your tongue from evil."

The entire book deals with this single subject, expounding the enormous dimensions of evil which lie in the evil tongue.

Published in 1873, the work was followed by five other books by the author, dealing with various aspects of the same subject. In those books the rabbi enumerated no less than thirty-one Torah prohibitions an individual is liable to transgress by engaging in *lashon ha-ra*. He also outlined numerous possible scenarios in which a person may commit the sin of evil utterance—sometimes totally unaware that he was doing anything wrong. One instance which he did not enumerate in his books comes from a story told about him:

One day, the story is told, the Hafetz Hayim journeyed from the big city of Warsaw to the small town of Radeen where he lived. On the train he got into conversation with the man next to him who was also going to Radeen. "I am going," his fellow traveler announced, "to try to get a blessing from the famous saint, the great scholar, the author of the Hafetz Hayim." The rabbi felt uneasy hearing those flattering words and said: "You are most likely mistaken. The person you are going to is not much of a saint or scholar." The stranger became enraged at his ignorant and insolent interlocuter, a slightly-built, little man in poor man's clothing, and he angrily slapped his face. The elderly sage kept silent and did not react.

How shocked was the enthusiast upon arriving in town and making his way to the house of the Hafetz Hayim to find here the very person whose face he had slapped. He fell to his feet crying and begging for his forgiveness. The Hafetz Hayim however smiled at him good-heartedly: "You should not have to beg for my forgiveness. On the contrary, it is I who owe you thanks for teaching me a new important lesson on the very same subject with which I have dealt all my life. I learned from you that one should beware not only against slandering others, but should not even slander himself. I made a derogatory statement about myself to you, but was punished on the spot for doing so. Thank you."

Hafetz Hayim died in 1934 at the age of 95. Almost to the end of his days, he travelled from town to town, spreading his message of guarding against an evil tongue.

Life and Death

THE DEDICATION OF the tabernacle—what an exciting event! Only a short time ago, they were still slaves and now this colorful and elaborate structure, dedicated in a thrilling ceremony, planned to the most minute detail by Moses, the liberator and teacher. The dedication ceremony was performed by a magnificently clad Aaron and his handsome young sons. A soul-stirring pageant.

"And there came down fire from before the Lord . . . and when all the people saw it, they shouted and fell on their faces" (*Leviticus 9:24*). They sensed the *Shekhina*, the presence of the Lord, amongst them.

And then calamity strikes.

Nadab and Abihu, the two young priestly princes, who were just now so gracefully assisting their father in the dedication ritual, are carried out from the sanctuary, dead.

Aaron, their father, was stunned. Moses, the boys' uncle, undoubtedly was also pained at the sight. He announces that the lives of the young princes were taken because of wrongful deeds. He orders the dedication celebrations to continue and delegates Elazar and Ithamar, the younger brothers of the deceased, to go ahead with the ceremonies.

For generations to come there would still be discussions as to what actually was the sin committed by Nadab and Abihu for which they paid with their lives. Had they entered the sanctuary while drunk? A cardinal offense in the Israelite sanctuary, as this was an essential difference between the Israelite and the pagan places of worship, where drunkenness and fornication were often part of the ritual. Or had they entered those parts of the sanctuary "off limits" for them, the holy of holies?

Some sages in the Midrash suggested that Nadab and Abihu died not because of any particular misbehavior that day, but because of their attitude towards the high office they held.

The procession leading to the tabernacle was headed by Moses and Aaron, immediately followed by the rest of the Israelites. Seeing this, the young men presumably were filled with conceit and ambition and said to each other (one rabbi says they only thought so in their hearts): Pretty soon those two old guys will be dead, and we shall take over. They were too impatient to wait their turn and showed it. Said the Lord to them: "Boast not thyself of tomorrow" (*Proverbs 27:1*). Did you hear about "the young colts whose skins became rugs on their mothers' backs?"

Rabbi Levi, a third-century Palestinian sage, says they died because of the pain they caused the young girls who anticipated marrying them. In their inflated egos, Nadab and Abihu preferred bachelorhood to nice, eligible maidens. They said: "Look at us, our uncle on our father's side is king (Moses), and on our mother's side, chief of his tribe (Nahshon); our father is the high priest, and we ourselves are the highly esteemed deputies to the high priest. Where is there a young woman who merits marrying us?"

Where did their arrogance lead them? The answer is to be found in the book of Psalms (*78:63*): "Fire devoured their young men (why? because:) their maidens had no marriage song."

Despite the death of Nadab and Abihu, the dedication of the tabernacle and life went on, but surely, it was not the same. The catastrophe left its imprint on future events. The fact that there was a holocaust on the day of the dedication of the sanctuary could not be passed over unnoticed. Life would indeed go on even after the holocaust, but would never be the same again. Business, yes, but not as usual. A lesson many Jewish ideologies and organizations have not learned unfortunately even after the Holocaust that befell our people in our own day.

"The Lord spoke unto Moses after the death of the two sons of Aaron, when they drew near before the Lord and died" (*Leviticus 16:1*).

"After the death of the two sons of Aaron" is not written merely to mark the time when the Lord spoke to Moses. It marks the watershed between the "before" and the "after" of the ominous event.

Their death, and, in fact, the death of anyone dear to us, should not leave us cold and indifferent. We should not try to overlook or suppress it. The Torah and halakhic laws of mourning teach us that death must be taken realistically, without either self-deception or glorification; that we must not only learn to live with it, but also learn from it what we can.

Facing death, we must not be shocked into brooding self-pity or futile anger, but ask ourselves, what Rabbi Soloveitchik calls "the halakhic question," namely, now that it happened, that it is a fact, as gloomy a fact as it is, where do I go from here? What am I supposed *to do* now?

"After the death of the sons of Aaron" comes a long list of "conclusions" (*Leviticus 16–19*). They include the prohibition against intoxication while worshipping God, a detailed moral code in sexual matters and, eventually, a prescription for a life of holiness, which gives meaning to the span of our years spent on this earth.

The Torah portion that opens with the death of the sons

of Aaron is named "After Death" and includes the warning, or if you will, the promise: "Ye shall therefore keep my statutes and my judgments, which if a person does, he shall live in them" (*Leviticus 18:5*). This phrase *v'hai bahem* "he shall live in them," has become a cornerstone in the development of the halakhic principle (*pikuah nefesh*) that the laws of Torah are to be life-giving and are abrogated when they result in the opposite or are endangering life.

Job, a biblical hero, facing disaster and death, says (*1:21*): "Naked came I out of my mother's womb, and naked shall I return thither; the Lord gave and the Lord has taken away; blessed be the name of the Lord." These words of blessing for the Lord who gives and takes away are incorporated into the liturgy of theodicy (*ziduk ha-din*) upon a death.

Is that really all there is to it? Is man capable of blessing God equally for the giving as for the taking? My great teacher, Yehuda Ibn Shmuel, a profound, insightful scholar and in his personal life a suffering Job in Jerusalem, offered the following reading of this verse in Job: "The Lord gave, and the Lord has taken away, blessed be the name of the Lord for the years in between the giving and the taking away." Life takes on a different meaning as a blessed gift when viewed from this vantage point.

All You Need Is Love

ONE OF THE best-known, most often quoted verses in the Bible is: "Love your neighbor as yourself" (*Leviticus 19:18*). It is usually taken out of context. It is also not without problems when you come to look at it closely.

When two thousand years ago a Gentile came to Hillel, a Jerusalem rabbi of that time, requesting to be taught all of Judaism "while standing on one foot"—(he was not, I suppose, practising acrobatics; what he meant was, most likely, to be taught all of Judaism that stands "on one foot," namely, the one unifying principle upon which all of it is based)—Hillel, in response, quoted to him the commandment of love, translating it into the negative: "Do not do unto others, what you do not want to be done to yourself" (*TB Shabbat 31a*). Why did the great rabbi change the commandment from the positive to the negative? Was it his way in trying to cope with some of the problematics of the verse, something which rabbis and commentators throughout the ages tried to do?

About one hundred years after Hillel, Rabbi Akiva, perhaps the greatest rabbi of all generations, echoed the words of Hillel in suggesting (this time not to an impatient outsider, but for internal consumption) that "love your neighbor as yourself" is the "great rule," or the "all-inclusive principle," or if you wish, "the totality" (*klal gadol*) of the entire Torah (*JT, Nedarim 9:4*).

Another rabbi, Ben Azai, a contemporary of Rabbi Akiva, argued that there was another biblical statement which superseded the one chosen by Akiva. In Ben Azai's view the "great rule" is in the verses (*Genesis 5:1-2*): "This is the book of the generations of Adam: In the day that God created Adam in the likeness of God He made him; male and female created He them." Did Ben Azai disagree with Rabbi Akiva, or did he merely wish to supplement and support his colleague's statement? What is sure is that he, Ben Azai, did not find the verse quoted by Rabbi Akiva to be sufficiently satisfying. Why?

This brings us again to the problematics inherent in what seems to be on the surface a plain, clearly stated statement. This problematic is in the content, as well as in the wording, of the great rule of love as it appears in the Torah.

In its context it is part of the prerequisites for the fulfillment of the commandment which opens chapter 19 of Leviticus: "You shall be holy, because I, the Lord your God, am holy!" Holiness, just as love, is put forward not as a slogan or lofty aspiration, but as a guideline in day-to-day living. The requirement of love appears 18 verses removed from the opening statement of the chapter. Love is not the beginning, or immediate result, of the desire to be holy, but its culmination, following a long series of commandments to be acted out in practical daily life that makes love possible and real.

It is indeed much easier to "love the whole world" than to love one's next-door neighbor with whom one has to live on a day-to-day basis. What is more, if love is understood as a profound emotion, as it is indeed understood in Scriptures ("with all thy heart, with all thy soul and with all thy might" [*Deuteronomy 6:5*] or "love is strong as death; many waters cannot extinguish love" [*Song of Songs, 8:6-7*]), how can it be commanded by legislation? Are emotions something over which the individual exercises control and can turn on or off at will?

These questions and others gave way to numerous interpretations of the text stating the great rule of love. Hillel's elaboration on the verse in the negative precept, not doing unto others what one does not wish to be done to him, is one of those interpretations, which takes into consideration the difficulties of both content and text. Love is not expressed emotionally only, but also in conduct: "like yourself," as you do not wish to be hurt by what others may do unto you (and you can tell exactly what this is)—do not do the same unto others!

Rabbi Akiva sets "love your neighbor" as the "great rule" of the entire Torah, namely, as the source and qualifying criterion for all other commandments. (A famous medieval authority masterfully showed in his book *Shnei Luhot Ha-Berit—SHILA*—how all 613 precepts are derived directly from the great rule).

Akiva's colleague, Ben Azai, is not satisfied with the *kamocha*, "as yourself"—what if a person does not like himself, should he therefore not like others? He preferred another verse, where the love for others stems from the fact that all human beings, each of them, are created in the "likeness of God." Love of others is not to be dependant on love of oneself, but on the fact of each individual's God-given precious uniqueness. "Love your neighbor (or rather, your fellow human being) like yourself" meaning, *because* he is like yourself, created by God. No person has any more "rights" or privileges than the next person, emphasizes Ben Azai—whether in disagreement with Rabbi Akiva, whose "great rule" could be taken as applying only to one's own neighbor or clan, or supplementing the rationale for Rabbi Akiva's daring statement in declaring love of fellow humans as the totality of Torah.

Self-preservation, self-gratification, is the natural inclination of any living creature, humans included. Whoever heard of loving others for other than selfish reasons until the Bible of the Hebrews came and put before us the command of non-utilitarian love: love of God, of neighbor and of stranger? Altruistic love is an "invention" of Torah. The reason for loving our fellow human being is not for the sake of being loved, it is because "I am the Lord!" God Himself is love and humans deserve to be loved because they were created in His image; because every other human being is *kamocha*, just like you. A person, not a number. An original, not a carbon copy.

How can love be commanded? Many commentators do not interpret the passage as referring to emotions. They point out that in loving one's neighbor the grammatical form is not *v'ahavta et* (as it is in the love of God) "you should love Him," but *ve-ahavta le-raiakha*, which can be translated as "You shall be loving towards your fellow human" with the focus on deeds and behavior rather than on feelings. Hillel's negative formulation was presented in the Code of Maimonides in a positive manner: Do unto others what you would like to be done unto you! The rabbis in the Mishna (the ancient code of Jewish law) elaborate: Let other people's possessions be as precious to you as your own. As you would not want yours to be wasted, do not waste others. Let others' dignity be as safeguarded, as you wish yours to be. Do not violate other people's dignity, self-esteem or right to hold their own views. This is the Torah source for pluralism, which, I believe, is a basic Jewish concept.

The mystics of the Kabbala, who in the 16th century established their center in Safed in Galilee, introduced a special meditation to be recited before each prayer. It says: "I am hereby ready and prepared to fulfil the commandment to love thy fellow human as thyself." Only then was one considered worthy to face God in prayer. Hassidism, which grew out of the Kabbala in centuries following, raised the banner of love of neighbor higher, making it one of its major tenets. "I wish I could love"—said the Baal-Shem-Tov, the founder of Hassidism—"the most pious person, as much as God loves the most wicked person." It does not take much effort to love good people, nice people. The test of the fulfillment of the commandment is in loving those who are not as good and lovable in one's eyes. "Love your fellow human—as yourself," as you accept yourself with all your faults and shortcomings, accept others the same way.

In a somewhat humorous vein one modern rabbi interpreted the passage thus: "Love your fellow human like yourself," who is *like yourself*, in the same profession and line of business. It is easy for a rabbi to love a physician, for a lawyer to love a carpenter, or for an accountant to love a businessman. What Torah tells us is that we must learn to love people who are "like ourselves," working in the same area: Let one rabbi like another rabbi, one lawyer another lawyer, one businessman another, one secretary another, and so on. That does not come by itself. On that we have to be commanded. And then we must try hard to live up to the commandment.

At the End of the Road

"YOU SHALL BE HOLY"—holiness as an accessible human goal is at the center of the book of Leviticus, or if you wish, of the entire Torah. All the rest is commentary: the details of how to prepare ourselves for it and implement it in our lives.

Holiness is the Jewish answer to the problem of human existence. Mankind has always sought to ascribe some metaphysical meaning to physical life, suggesting that if man is not somehow *more* than human, he is *less* than human. Thus, attempts to transcend temporal life through art, eros, religion and immortality. Judaism taught that it is holiness that can add this extra dimension to our lives, not by escaping from life, but rather by striving to "be holy" in this world and in this life.

Many of the laws spelled out in the Torah combine together to serve as a practical day-to-day manual on how to live a life of holiness, for both layman and priest.

In the face of the fascination with death in ancient (and modern) religions, with man looking to temple and priest for "pie in the sky when you die," we find the following command:

"The Lord said to Moses, speak to the priests, the sons

of Aaron and say to them: None shall defile himself for any dead person among his people" (*Leviticus* 21:1).

This command must be seen against the background of the gaudy worship of the dead in ancient Egypt, from where the people of Israel had recently emerged. All of life in ancient Egypt centered around death, concentrating on the building of one's "house of eternity," the tomb. When death came, the priests, gods and goddesses took over with a series of rituals, processions and incantations to get the body to its proper place. The dead were buried with clothes, eating utensils, weapons and other personal articles. In the royal burials of the first dynasty, slaves were slain and buried by the king's side to serve him in the next world.

Of course, not everyone could afford the full "services" of the priests at such occasions. It was a privilege reserved for royalty and the very rich. Funerals were "big business" for temple and priest and the extensive death industry that grew around them.

Not only is the Israelite priest restrained from all this, he is not allowed even to come near the dead. This emphasizes the fact that his job is not to cater to the dead, but to serve as a teacher and model of holiness for the living. In fact, he is "defiled" by any contact with the dead, a practice still in force today. A traditional Jew who is a *cohen* (a descendent of the family of Aaron) may not enter a cemetery or a house where there is a corpse.

However, to eliminate the suggestion that there is an intrinsic demonic defilement in the human corpse, from which the servants of the Lord must keep away, comes the exception which sheds light on the rule. The priest may (according to the interpretation of Rabbi Akiva: *must*) take care of the burial of seven of his close kin, which are: his wife, father, mother, son, daughter, brother and sister.

Taking care of the dead and seeing to their burial is considered a prime human obligation. Thus the *cohen* cannot hide behind his priestly cloak to shirk his responsibilities towards his close relatives or for that matter towards a lonely poor person (*met mitzva*) whom no one else will bother burying. It is not death that defiles the priest, but the shifting of the weight of his duties from the living to the dead.

It is because of respect for life on this earth that the taking care of the dead is accorded a high priority in one's religious duties. The burial of the dead was not handled in Jewish tradition by professional undertakers who may grow coarse in doing their job. Every Jewish community had a volunteer group who would consider it their honorable duty to care for the dead and the bereaved. They were known as the *hevra kadisha*, the holy society. They did not consider death a fascinating phenomenon, but rather a grim fact of life which awaits all of us and some of us must be prepared to deal with it.

Funerals in ancient Egypt lasted seventy days: they were filled with pomp and ceremony. In Jewish tradition, the less time that elapses between death and burial, the better. The simpler the affair, the more commendable. The ancient tradition in Jerusalem is not to leave the dead unburied even overnight. Funerals are therefore held during the night, if death occurs late in the day, and there is no special reason for delaying the funeral.

The rabbi, as the ancient priest of old, has no specific religious function at a funeral. He does not "lead" the deceased to his eternal rest. The only religious duty is to recite the *kaddish* prayer, which in no way is a prayer for the dead, but a call to the living.

The *kaddish* is the rare exception in Jewish liturgy where the prayer is not directed towards God, but to the audience present. It declares that even at this moment of grief and loss, in the face of the helplessness and defeat demonstrated by death, we reaffirm the fact that the purpose of life in this world is that God's name be magnified and sanctified—"in this world which He has created according to His will," and that the kingdom of God may be established "in your lifetime and during your days, and within the life of the entire House of Israel, speedily and soon."

Not in the afterlife is God's great name to be magnified and sanctified ("The dead cannot praise the Lord," *Psalm 115*; compare also *Psalm 30*), but in this world and in this life.

When Torah and Land Meet

THE MARVELLOUS EVENT at Mount Sinai is well behind us. The biblical narrative has, since then, covered a long and trying road: the tabernacle has been built and dedicated and numerous laws have been introduced in detail. Now, quite unexpectedly, as we reach the 25th chapter of Leviticus, the Torah brings us back to Mount Sinai:

"And the Lord spoke to Moses on Mount Sinai, saying: Speak to the children of Israel and say to them: when you come into the land which I give you, then shall the land keep a Sabbath unto the Lord" (*Leviticus 25:1–2*).

Ma inyan shmita etzel har sinai?"—what are the sabbatical laws doing at Mount Sinai? ask the ancient rabbis.

One possible explanation is that by the introduction at this point in the scripture of the law pertaining to the land, namely, that of the Sabbatical and Jubilee year, emphasis is being laid on the fact that the revelation at Sinai, where we received the Torah and the commandments, had one aim: the building of a model society by the people of Israel in their only real, sovereign land.

The exalted moral code of Mount Sinai was not intended to guide a rootless cosmopolitan individual, but a whole people living on its land and cultivating it. The juxtapostion, after a long interval, of the event at Sinai and the life of the land serves as a twofold reminder: firstly, that the ideals of the Torah must not remain in the lofty realm of the abstract, but should be realized on the soil of the land itself; and secondly that this land is more than a mere geopolitical or agro-economic entity—it is also capable of celebrating the Sabbath, and expected to do so.

Just as a human being possesses an "extra soul" which finds expression on the Sabbath, so the land, too, in its own way is entitled to its Sabbath (*verses 2-6*).

This Sabbath of the land and the Jubilee year which comes in it wake are considered by many thinkers to be among the most advanced social reforms in history. They protect society against the evils of feudalism and totalitarianism, assuring an inherent "liberty to all the inhabitants in the land" (*verse 10*) and the right of each individual to "return to his home and to his family."

These reforms can be carried out only when Torah and Land meet, when the "children of Israel come to the land which I give you."

The choice of *Haftara* (the reading from the prophets)— Jeremiah chapter 32—which accompanies this portion of the Torah, is no less telling in showing that land, "down-to earth" as it is, is capable of conveying the most important spiritual messages.

If the Torah reading presents a message of freedom and equality, the prophetic reading offers us a message of hope, manifested even in the darkest moments of despair.

Jerusalem was under heavy siege by the Babylonian armies for the third consecutive year. The enemy troops on the ramps were attacking the city from all sides; within the city too, the sword, famine and plague raged.

Jeremiah the prophet had been thrown into jail by the king, Zedekiah, who was angered by his public pronouncements that the city was about to fall into the hands of the enemy and the king himself taken into captivity.

And then, while still in jail, Jeremiah announced that "the word of the Lord" had told him that Hanamel, his cousin, would come to him suggesting that he buy a field in Anatot (today Anata outside Jerusalem, near Shuafat).

Hanamel, in fact, did come and offered the field for sale and Jeremiah, forewarned by God, completed the transaction, paying Hanamel seventeen shekels of *silver*. The deed was signed in public for everyone to see and ostentatiously deposited with Jeremiah's secretary, Baruch Ben Neriah.

At this point, after getting all the attention he wanted in his purchasing of the field, Jeremiah made the following public statement:

"For this is what the Lord Almighty, the God of Israel says: Houses, fields and vineyards will again be bought in this land" (32:15).

Jeremiah was not fooling himself, nor did he intend to fool others concerning the gravity of the situation. Wasn't he the one who had been imprisoned because of his pessimistic forecasts? Yet—unlike some latter-day opinion-molders—he wanted to impress upon his people not only the reality of impending doom, but also the hope of eventual triumph.

Seventeen silver shekels (estimated at seven ounces or 200 grams of silver) was probably not a large sum of money at that time. But it was not the size of the investment which was important; it was Jeremiah's readiness to invest in land in circumstances which made that land appear utterly worthless. The seventeen shekels represented a tangible investment in the future of the land and of the people.

Yet, it was not Jeremiah who emerged the hero of the day, but his all-but-forgotten cousin, Hanamel. Jeremiah was told how to act by God; he merely followed orders. Hanamel, on the other hand, was no prophet, but a simple citizen, one of the rank and file of the people.

That he was ready at such a time to do business in real estate with his cousin the prophet was proof, even for Jeremiah himself, that the battle over the land had not been lost. It was then, when Hanamel appeared, that Jeremiah said (*verse 8*): "*I knew,* this was the word of the Lord."

Jeremiah could easily have suspected that his cousin was only after the silver shekels. He did not, however, resort to suspicion and mudslinging. Instead, he considered Hanamel a hero, seeing in him a true representative of the people, one who does not despair under the worst circumstances. Indeed, inspired by Hanamel, Jeremiah prophesies about the future, encouraging more investments in this threatened land: "Houses, fields and vineyards will again be bought in this land!"

Jeremiah himself was troubled by doubts, which he expressed in his prayer to God (*32:16–25*). But his doubts were silenced as God replied: (*verse 27*): "I am the Lord, the God of all mankind. Is anything too hard for me?"

The way from Sinai to the Land might be long and arduous. But it is one of freedom and equality, faith and hope.

Strength and Peace

A SINGLE WORD, it has been said, has sometimes lost or won an empire. There is a single word in the Torah that has caused a whole new world of moral and religious thought. It is a short word, consisting of just two letters, the word "if."

"If" introduces the covenantal imperative, establishing an inevitable interdependence between Israel's destiny and moral conduct.

Notwithstanding the long-standing special relationship that exists between God and his chosen people, Israel does not enjoy any special privileges. No protekzia. The blessings Israel is to receive are conditional.

"If you follow my decrees and are careful to obey my commandments—I will send you rain in its season" and all other blessings that follow (*Leviticus 26:3–13*). "But if you will not listen to me . . . and if you reject my decrees . . . then I will do this to you," and a long list of curses follows (*ibid.,14–43*).

The fateful "if" always stands between Israel and the normal desire for power and prosperity that it shares with other nations. This is however only one aspect of the nature of the covenant between God and his people. Another

· aspect follows and that is, according to the divine promise, no matter how far Israel would be dispersed and how
greatly it would suffer, it would never be completely abandoned by God. Eventually there must come a reconciliation between God and his people. "Yet, in spite of this, I
will not abhor them so as to destroy them completely,
breaking my covenant with them, I am the Lord their
God" (*verse* 44).

This comforting note at the end of the long threatening
list of curses led many a Torah commentator throughout
the ages to find hints of consolation and promise even in
between the lines of the curses themselves. They interpreted the curses as being blessings in disguise.

The most famous of these is the threat of the land being
laid waste and remaining thus, even after the enemies
had taken it over, as they "shall be appalled by it" (26:32).
Although Israel was to be driven out of its land, no other
nation would ever strike roots in it, as this might create
"new facts" which might prevent Israel's returning to the
land. It is a historical empirical fact—maintains Rabbi
Moses ben Nahman (Nahmanides) after immigrating to
Palestine in the 12th century—that no other nation has
ever succeeded in bringing back the land to its former
bloom. It is as if the land insisted on waiting for its rightful owners to come back.

This remained true also for the following seven centuries. Conquering powers came and went. None of them
conquered the wasteland. Its barren hills and swamp-
ridden valleys did not begin to bloom again until the return of the Jews only a hundred years ago, with the first
colonization efforts of the Yishuv and the Zionist movement.

Another blessing in disguise was found by a contemporary rabbi, turning over one of the most dreadful and horrifying of the curses to its brighter, more cheerful side.
The verse reads: "You will eat the flesh of your sons

and the flesh of your daughters" (*26:29*). That, too, could be interpreted as a blessing in disguise, meaning that observant parents could visit and eat meat in the homes of their sons and daughters without having to worry whether the food is kosher. . . .

While the detailed aspects of the curses are described in 25 verses (*14–43*) and the blessings are concentrated in only 11 verses (*3–13*), it is obvious that the weight and promise of the blessings is predominant. There is no need to enumerate details when describing the ultimate good a nation should strive for.

This is the order of the good life as we follow its appearance in the Torah: 1) economic prosperity arising from one's own self-sufficient land, not depending on import; 2) security, freedom from fear; 3) peace in the land; 4) strength and valor to overcome one's enemies; 5) increase of population in numbers through high birth rate and aliya; and, finally the acme of all aspirations: 6) God's presence among the people.

The order of priorities is somewhat perplexing, with the blessing of peace apparently in the wrong place.

Rashi (1040–1105), the classic commentator on the Torah, suggests that peace is deliberately given a place in the center to teach us that economic prosperity, and even guaranteed secure borders, are worthless if there is no peace. "Where there is peace, there is everything; no peace, nothing." Rashi does not resolve the puzzle why strength and the ability to chase the enemy come after security and peace and not, as would logically fit, before achieving those.

Ibn Ezra (1093–1167) seems to respond to this question with one word that he adds after the phrase "I will grant peace": *beinechem*, meaning, among you. The strength to drive off your enemies would come if there first be internal peace and unity among you.

Others find in the order of the components of the good life as it appears in Torah insights into the meaning of peace. Everyone is, of course, for peace, but not everyone knows how to get it or make sure that it is lasting. To ensure that peace prevails, a nation must make sure that its enemies do not misinterpret its desire for peace as a sign of weakness. Peace would be secured permanently if the enemies know that the nation is properly prepared for war and capable of deterring any would-be assailant, even when it is outnumbered by enemy forces. "I will grant peace in the land and you shall lie down untroubled by anyone" (26:6). When? When your enemies would be convinced (*verses 7,8*) that five of you are capable of chasing a hundred of them, and a hundred of you, ten thousand of them.

The same sentiment is expressed also in the Psalms (*29:11*):

"The Lord gives strength to his people; the Lord blesses his people with peace."

The Psalmist too understood that strength is a prerequisite for peace. Where there is no strength, peace will not last. Peace and strength must go together.

במדבר

NUMBERS

וַיָּבֹאוּ עַד־נַחַל אֶשְׁכֹּל וַיִּכְרְתוּ מִשָּׁם
זְמוֹרָה וְאֶשְׁכּוֹל עֲנָבִים אֶחָד וַיִּשָּׂאֻהוּ
בַמּוֹט בִּשְׁנָיִם

And they came to the wadi of
Eshkol, and cut down from thence a
branch with one cluster of grapes,
and they carried it between two on a
pole;

Numbers 13:23

True People's Army

JEWISH TRADITION CHANGED the ancient name of the fourth book of Torah from the Book of Numbers (*humash ha-pekudim*) to *Bamidbar,* meaning, in the wilderness. This change from the original name (mentioned in Mishna Yoma 7,1 and still preserved in most Bible translations) is not without significance.

The Israelites' sojourn in the desert for no less than forty years seems to be a most important phase in their march from bondage to freedom. If Exodus became forever a paradigm for liberation, the interim stay in the wilderness is no less exemplary. The book *Bamidbar* teaches us that there are no short-cuts to the Promised Land, and no instant transformation from bands of liberated slaves into a responsible, self-governing nation; no generation of redemption (*dor geula*) without a generation dying out in the desert (*dor ha-midbar*) preceding it.

The commencement of the reading of the book of *Bamidbar* in the synagogue is almost always on the Sabbath before *Shavuot,* marking the giving of Torah on Mount Sinai. That the Torah was given at Sinai, in the wilderness, called forth numerous interpretations in Judaic thought. The best-known of these is that God chose to give the Torah in no-man's land, to show that it does not belong to any one people or land, but is free for anyone who is ready to accept it. The location of the Revelation in no-man's land proclaims, according to this interpretation, the universality of Torah.

Other interpretations read different messages in the link between Torah and the wilderness. All emphasize that the wilderness location is not accidental, but part of the significance of Torah and redemption. The desert was not seen, however, as in certain religions, as an ideal site for meditative closeness to God and an escape to pristine monastic life. On the contrary, Torah was meant to be lived in the midst of civilization, its function to conquer and curb the demonic wilderness within man.

Revelation in the desert serves as a constant reminder that if man does not overcome the desert, the desert may eventually overcome him. There is no peaceful co-existence between the two, either in the physical or spiritual realms.

The protracted lingering in the wilderness served for the children of Israel as an intensive schooling in preparation for entering the land of their destination. Their trials and tribulations are told in detail in the 33 chapters of *Bamidbar*. The wilderness became thus not only the locale where Torah was given, but also part of Torah itself.

The first act Moses is ordered to undertake, as the story of the Israelites in the desert unfolds, is to take a census of all adult males "twenty years old and upward, all that are able to go to war" (*Numbers 1:3*). Why an army? Weren't they used to the miracles wrought by God and Moses, His faithful messenger? He who subdued their fierce enemies in Egypt, He who split the sea for them—isn't He going to help them reach their destination as He had promised time and time again?

Of course, He is going to help them, but the lesson they must learn at this point, as they are preparing to go to their own land, is that one must not rely on miracles alone. In fact, one is not allowed by Jewish law to rely on miracles (*Bab. Talmud, Kidushin 39b*). To benefit from the miraculous help of God, Israel, as an independent nation in its own land, must have a well-trained, well-equipped army.

The army to be formed was not to be merely a token military force, comprised of a select group only, but to include each and every able member of the congregation of Israel "from twenty years old and upward." A true people's army.

This represents quite a revolutionary idea for the ancient world. Israel is usually credited with heralding the ideas of liberty, equality and the like. The fact that Israel is also the originator of a new revolutionary military concept is hardly known.

Yet, indeed, this is history's first record of an army that is composed neither of slaves or mercenaries, nor of volunteers or professional soldiers, but rather an entire people. Everyone, without exception, if eligible by age, is to be conscripted. Everyone serves equally, and men for all the ranks are provided by the people.

Total compulsory conscription is generally considered a recent innovation. It was not found in ancient times in Assyria, Babylon, Egypt, Greece, or Rome. It was unknown during medieval times, when the responsibility to fight for one's people or country was divided between the commanding noblemen and the commanded masses of slaves. The first instance in which we find an entire people sharing equal responsibility for its military duties is with the children of Israel, in the desert.

The army formed in the desert was yet in another sense to be a true people's army in contrast to a militaristic fighting force. As Moses is about to take the census for the purpose of forming the army, he is told: "Take ye the sum of all the congregation of Israel by their families, by their fathers' houses, according to the number of names" (*Numbers 1:2*). The Israeli soldier is not to become a mere nameless number; he must remain always an individual with an individual name. He must never become an anonymous G.I., but must always remain part of his family and father's house. A soldier-fighter in time of need, a son and family man, all the time.

What a Blessing

"THUS SHALL YOU bless the people of Israel, say to them: The Lord bless you and keep you. The Lord radiate his face towards you and be gracious unto you. The Lord lift up his countenance towards you and grant you peace" (*Numbers 6:23–26*).

The above, known as the "three-fold priestly blessing" and pronounced to this day in the synagogue service, is perhaps the oldest liturgical formula known to us.

"Thus"—in fifteen well-measured, terse Hebrew words, no more and no less—"shall you bless the people of Israel."

Against the background of saints, sorcerors, and magicians in the ancient temples, Torah comes to make clear that the blessing originates not from the priest, but from God himself. The priest is not expected to pour out his superfluity of blessings. All he has to do is to "put My Name upon the people of Israel" by enunciating the prescribed three-fold formula, fifteen words and no more, "and I (God himself) will bless them" (*ibid., verse 27*).

What is the nature of this all-encompassing blessing? And why is it given in three parts? Many generations have offered answers, reflecting not only their own dreams and fears in the quest for blessing, but also keen efforts to understand the blessing from the point of view of God and Torah. What emerges from most interpretations is that the three parts of the priestly benediction correspond to three distinct areas.

In the beginning there is the blessing for material goods; second, the blessing on our intellectual endeavors; and third, on our mental and spiritual well-being.

The priests are given specific instructions as to the order and exact wording of the blessing. Given their own vantage point in the holiness of the temple, they might assume that the divine blessing should be confined to spirituality and godliness. The given formula of the benediction brings them down to earth and reminds them that people need proper material conditions as a prerequisite for engaging in lofty spiritual pursuits.

"The Lord bless you," the ancient Midrash interpolates here: *be-mamon*, with money. "And keep you"—*min ha-mazikim*, keep you away from the destroyers, damagers, spoilers, pests, and demons.

"It is not so good with money, as it is bad without it," my mother, may she be healthy and strong, often says. Rashi in his commentary asks: What good is there in being blessed with money if eventually robbers come and take it away from you? That is why "the Lord bless you" (with money) must be accompanied with "and keep you," so the the money is not taken away from you. There are, as we know, a million ways of making money, a million and one for losing it.

The "robbers" Rashi talks about are not necessarily tough highway gunmen. They may chase you under different guises, as overreaching tax collectors, phony fund-raisers, make-believe investment consultants, faddist health advisors, status-selling PR experts, soft-spoken piety peddlers, and many others. All these "damagers" are constantly after you, as the Lord blesses you with money. He must therefore also "keep you" and protect you against all those false well-wishers.

Another way of looking at the dual expressions of "bless you" and "keep you" is offered by a number of commentators:

May God "bless you" with possessions and "keep you" from those possessions possessing you. Money can corrupt your personality and your patterns of living. It can make you forget family and friends. It can alienate you from your traditions. "May the Lord bless you" with money, but may He also "keep you" from all the damages money might bring on you, now that you have been blessed with it.

The Talmud (*Baba Bathra* 7b), tells about a pious man with whom Elijah the prophet used to meet regularly. As the man prospered and built a fence and fancy gate around his house, Elijah stopped appearing to him and explained that with this new addition to his house, the man made himself inaccessible to the poor crying for help. Elijah would not approve of the "new style" money brings with it—double-locked doors, receptionists and secretaries, sophisticated intercom systems and uniformed doormen.

Another emphasis on the link between the "blessing" and the "keeping" is the following: "May the Lord bless you" with money, and may He "keep you" from accumulating this money in non-proper ways (like theft, desecration of the Sabbath, etc.). May the money that you would be blessed with always be clean and kosher.

The radiance of God's face upon you, which enables

you to share his grace, is the content of the second part of the three-fold benediction. God shines to us and through us in the light of Torah and wisdom. "A person's wisdom illuminates his face" (*Ecclesiastes 8:1*). Material abundance and understanding of Torah and life combine together to complete the blessing, with the Lord lifting his countenance unto you and granting you perfection (*shalom-shalem* = perfect) and peace of mind.

This understanding of the three-fold priestly benediction is reflected as well in the benediction invoked by the priests of the ancient sect in the Judean desert on all who joined their community. It is found in the Manual of Discipline of the Dead Sea Scrolls and reads as follows:

> May the Lord bless you with all good
> and keep you from all evil
> May He illumine your heart with insight
> into the things of life
> and grace you with knowledge
> of things eternal
> May He lift up his gracious countenance
> towards you
> to grant you peace everlasting.

On Complaining

THERE ARE MANY cases in which translations do not do justice to the original Hebrew of the Torah. It does not say (*Numbers 11:1*), "And when the people complained" (as in the authorized King James version), nor that "the people took to complaining bitterly" (as in the new JPS version). *"Vayehi ha-am k'mitonenim"* could simply be rendered: and the people were *like* complainers, or murmurers.

They were not complaining loud and clear, only murmuring "like" complainers. No one heard their complaint, nor are we told what it was all about. "They were *like* complainers and (that is why only) the Lord heard it and his anger was kindled."

In principle, God is not angry at people who complain when they have good cause for doing so. God was not angered even when the complaint was voiced with the most strident words: "would we had died in the land of Egypt when we sat at the fleshpots and when we did eat bread to the full: for ye have brought us forth into the wilderness, to kill this whole assembly with hunger" (*Exodus 16:3*).

The Lord did not punish them on account of these harsh words. On the contrary, he responded by showering them with bread from heaven (*ibid., verse 4*).

This was not the only time when the Israelites had complained and received a positive response to their grievance. In Marah (*Exodus 15:23–25*), the water was bitter "and the people murmured against Moses, saying, what shall we drink? And the Lord showed Moses a tree, which when he had cast into the waters, these waters were made sweet."

Again in Rephidim (*ibid., 17:1–7*) "the people thirsted for water and murmured against Moses and said, 'Wherefore is this, that thou has brought us up out of Egypt, to kill us and our children and our cattle with thirst.' " And again, the Lord responded to their grumbling and brought forth water from the rock.

Here, in the desert, in Tabera, we face a different situation. The people are not complaining about some specific problem. They actually have everything they need and grumble for the sake of grumbling. "And Moses heard the people weeping family by family" (*Numbers 11:10*). Murmuring, bewailing, moaning, fretting, and whining became a family pastime. Every social gathering led to weeping and lamenting. "*Mitonenim*" could also be understood (*see Nachmanides*) as mourning their own death. This kind of complaining aroused God's anger and brought Moses, the humble and patient leader, to the point of despair. "Why have you brought this trouble upon your servant? What have I done to displease you that you put the burden of all these people on me? . . . If this is how you are going to treat me, put me to death right now, if I have found favor in your eyes, and do not let me face my own ruin!"

When the people levelled justifiable complaints concerning food and water, God was on their side and helped them out of their predicament. Here it was the marginal "rabble," not the entire people, who were inciting the people to murmur.

To go back again to the original Hebrew: "And the riff-raff among them craved a craving" (*verse 4*). It is only afterwards that this craving takes on the form of "Who shall give us meat to eat?" In the beginning it is the "craving" itself that they are craving. Bored with the affluent life, they were seeking ever new thrills and new cravings to titillate and stimulate them.

Too demoralized to look towards the future, they turn to the past. "We remember the fish which we did eat in Egypt freely." Every person and his memories. Tell me what you remember and I will tell you who you are. Their memory was very selective indeed. They did not remember the torture and humiliation of slavery, they did not remember the joys and excitements of liberation. All they remembered was the fish they ate in Egypt.

Their outcry is "Who shall give us meat to eat?" They are reminiscing about meat. Why suddenly do they "remember the fish"? And did they really get fish freely without pay? We know about the "generosity" of the Egyptians. Even straw to produce the bricks, they would not give them, says Rashi.

Rabbi Meir Simha Hacohen (1845–1926), famed author of the Torah commentary *Meshekh Hokhma*, makes an interesting point: We know that eating meat out of "craving" alone was prohibited for the children of Israel in the desert (*Deuteronomy 12*). All animals had to be ritually slaughtered. And the new laws of kashrut put so many restrictions on the eating of meat. What the complainers wanted was to be able to eat meat as "freely" as one eats fish, which does not require specific rules of slaughtering or koshering. Thus they were crying, "Who shall give us

flesh. . . . We remembered the fish we ate freely. Would
that we may consume meat as 'free' from restrictions as
we consume fish. . . ."

How was life in the country where you come from?"
The question was asked of a new immigrant, just arrived
in Israel from the USSR.
"I could not complain," was his answer.
"And how were your living quarters there?"
Again the same answer: "Well, I couldn't complain."
"And your standard of living?"
And again: "I couldn't complain."
"If everything was so swell, why then did you come
here?"
"Oh," replied the new *oleh*, "here, thank God, I *can*
complain!"
A free person in a free society may and should complain over wrongs. Sometimes God may be angry with
us, not because we complain, but because we do not complain enough. We must make sure, however, that our
complaints should not turn into murmuring for its own
sake, murmuring that looks "like" complaining, "*k'mitonenim*."
"*Vayehi ha-am k'mitonenim ra be'oznei hashem*"—the
wording in this opening verse is somewhat puzzling.
What does the word *ra*, evil or bad, refer to? Does it refer
to their complaining, or to the fact that it was displeasing
to God?
The answer, according to our understanding, is that
the obscure structure of the sentence comes to tell us
both: God was displeased and angered because their
complaining in this case was bad, groundless and totally
unjustified.

Pompous Delegation, Tragic End

"THE LORD SAID to Moses: Send some men to explore the land of Canaan, which I am giving the Israelites" (*Numbers 13:1*). Not only were the results of this expedition disastrous, as Torah goes on to tell us (*ibid.*, 2–22), but it was altogether ill-conceived and badly prepared. The idea to send spies to scout the promised land did not originate from God. When Moses re-tells the story (*Deuteronomy 1:22–40*) he reminds the Israelites that it was they who put pressure on him to set up an investigation commission to spy out the land. Their insecurity as to where they were going was a sign of disbelief in God.

Proper intelligence and reconnaissance work is a prerequisite for successful warfare. The Israelites too, at a later stage, when Joshua is about to attack Jericho, send men to spy the enemy territory (*Joshua 2*) even after having dismally failed in their first spying project.

What were the reasons for their failing now and their success later?

It seems that their demand to send spies to explore the land in the time of Moses was not part of the war effort. They did not want to learn as in the time of Joshua which is the best way to enter the land, but rather if it is worth going there altogether. If it is really the land of milk and honey they were promised. As if going to the land of Israel could be taken conditionally, saying: "I'll go—but first I must see if I like it there. . ."

The difference between the two expeditions is also in the manner in which they were composed. Joshua sent two men, anonymous secret agents, who camouflaged their identity hiding out in the house of a prostitute. The number of people sent by Moses was no less than twelve. Each tribe must have demanded to be represented on such an important mission. They were not anonymous undercover agents, but the "leaders of Israel." Their names were prominently listed, name and father's name, as befits such a distinguished leadership mission. Had the Torah been given with illustrations we surely would have been presented with their photographs as well.

It was no doubt beneath their dignity to lodge at the home of a poor prostitute. Don't distinguished leaders on a public mission deserve to stay in five-star hotels?

Kli Yakar, the popular Torah commentary by R. Ephrayim of Luntschitsz (1550–1619), finds one additional reason for the impending failure of the mission. The mission failed, the *Kli Yakar* suggests, because it was made up of men only and despite its enormous size, did not include even one woman. Had they followed the will of God, they would have sent on this mission women, "who know how to love the land of Israel, much more than the men."

Be that as it may, the episode of the *m'raglim* (the spies) remained a traumatic experience in the annals of the history of Israel. It sealed the fate of an entire generation to die in the wilderness without reaching the land of their destination. It was not without a profound effect on future generations as well.

The "spies" were asked to go to the land and return

with a report on what they saw. So they did. They did not lie or twist the facts as they saw them. They brought back a truthful report that no one contested. What then was so terrible about their acts which were so severely condemned?

It was because they overstepped the perimeters of their appointments. They were delegated to be a fact-finding mission and were given specific assignments (*verses 17–20*). Indeed, they spared no effort to carry out their assignment, went up and down the country, kept an open eye and registered everything they heard and saw. Upon returning they reported in detail about everything. So far so good. The tragic havoc was caused by adding to their otherwise objective report only one extra word!

"We went into the land to which you sent us", they told Moses, "and it does flow with milk and honey! Here is its fruit."

They buttressed their testimony with concrete evidence. Then they added one word: "But"—and continued their factual testimony—"The people who live there are powerful, and the cities are fortified and very large."

Had they left out the word "but", they would have stayed within the limits of a factual report. A land flowing with milk and honey, powerful people, fortified large cities, etc. When they added the word "but"—it was no more a factual account, but rather an attempt to sway public opinion. Yes . . . but.

The heated debate which ensued between the ten spies and the dissenting Caleb the son of Jepphune and Joshua the son of Nun, was not concerning the facts, which no one contested, but about the conclusions one is to draw from those facts.

The dramatic public debate brought out the subtle tendency of the spies to spread fear and panic among the people, while Caleb and Joshua combatted this tendency.

In their demoralizing campaign the spies keep men-
tioning the *anakim*, a dreadful breed of giants whose presence in the land of Canaan would make it impossible for
the Israelites to conquer the land. The repeated mention
of the *anakim* discourages the people, "takes out" their
hearts and "melts it away."

"We seemed like grasshoppers in our own eyes, and so
we looked the same to them" the spies announce (13:33).
When a person seems like nothing in his own eyes, comments a modern rabbi, he would look the same in the
eyes of others.

Joshua and Caleb did not contradict the facts as they
were presented in the majority report. In their dissent,
they refute the unhealthy attitude as to the ability of the
people to go into the land.

"The land we passed through to explore," they assert,
"is exceedingly good." The cities are indeed large and fortified, yet, there is no reason to fear them, nor the giant
anakim, "for they are *lahmeinu*, their strength is gone."
This word *"lahmeinu"* is usually translated "our bread,"
meaning we shall swallow them up as one swallows bread
(*Rashi*).

A more startling interpretation of *"lahmeinu"* is that it
comes from the same root as *milhama*, war. Thus, Joshua
and Caleb were not only boosting the people to regain
confidence in their own strength, they went further in
stating that as to the giant *anakim*, of which you are so
scared, they are *lahmeinu—our war*, we personally will take
care of them. We are not only arguing—we shall also act
and take on personal responsibility to prove our point.

How amazing that forty-five years later, as the land is
conquered by the Israelites we find that Joshua and 85-
year-old Caleb had not forgotten their commitment and
did actually take care personally of the *anakim*. The story
is told in detail in the book of Joshua, end of chapter 11,
and in one of the most moving narratives in the Bible in
the same book, chapter 14.

Disastrous Mutiny

KORAH WOULD HAVE certainly vanished into oblivion, as did almost all the 600,000 who came out of Egypt during the great Exodus, had it not been for the opposition party he formed in the desert. Korah contested the leadership of the "establishment" headed by Moses and Aaron. The Torah as interpreted in Jewish tradition does not hold this against Korah. But it does question the methods of, and the true motivation behind, this mutiny, which led the campaign to disaster.

Korah remains forever the prototype of the demagogue who knows how to stir up the masses skillfully. His arguments are ostensibly reasonable and just, but prove false and disastrous.

Korah appears to be arguing for a noble cause. He is the gallant champion of a more democratic society. He addresses Moses and Aaron saying: "Ye take too much upon you, seeing all the congregation are holy, every one of them, and the Lord is among them: whereof then lift ye up yourselves above the assembly of the Lord?" While Moses commands the people saying, "You shall be holy" and makes many demands of them in order that they should *become* holy, Korah says "everyone of them" *is*

holy. He propagates a "people's democracy." He makes
everybody happy.

He wages a campaign against the nepotism allegedly
practiced by Moses in the appointment of his brother
Aaron as high priest. He, Korah, is against the concentra-
tion of power at the top. "Ye take too much upon you."

He no doubt got a good press: most likely the entire
"mass media" was on his side. No wonder, then, that
"When Moses heard, he fell on his face."

As with all able demagogues, Korah's campaign gathers
momentum with the exploitation of every possible argument. The sages of the Midrash and the commentators of
the Torah in many generations elaborate on the tactics
he used.

First, the Midrash attempts to reveal the real motivation
for Korah's rebellion. Was he really wholeheartedly concerned to bring about a democratic society, or was there
something else? The sages of the Midrash are puzzled: if
Korah's case was good, why did his effort end in disaster?

The Midrash supplies data on Korah's past activities.
Self-appointed spokesman for "the poor and deprived
masses," he had been, prior to the Exodus, the treasurer
of Pharaoh. Although probably salaried, he did very well
for himself. In fact, he possessed treasures so vast that he
is said to have employed 300 mules to carry the keys to
them (to this day the favorite Yiddish expression for de-
noting fabulous wealth is *reich vie Korah*—as rich as
Korah).

What really spurred Korah's bitter rebellion was a personal grievance. He felt that Moses had overlooked him
when he made the appointment of chief of the Levite divi-
sion of Kohat. The prestigious job was given to Elizaphan,
a cousin of Korah. Korah thought he himself should have
gotten the job.

What started as a family fight (Korah, Moses, Aaron

and Elizaphan were first cousins), soon turned into a major political upheaval through the skillful manipulations of Korah. No less than "250 princes of the congregation" became involved, among them some leading members of the tribe of Reuben who, as Jacob's firstborn, must have felt hurt too. All the followers of Korah were promised key positions, if and when. . .

The multi-millionaire Korah was the natural representative of the princes and other rich people. But that did not prevent him from circulating a story he invented, according to the Midrash, to show the oppressive burden of Moses and Aaron on the poor masses.

"In my vicinity," Korah told, "there lived a widow with two daughters who owned a field whose yield was just sufficient to keep body and soul together. Whenever this woman tried to plough her field, to sow, to reap and so on, Moses or Aaron would always appear either to prevent her from doing what she intended, because it is forbidden by the law of the Torah, or to collect tithes and various taxations for the priests or the Levites."

Korah's campaign combined an outcry for democratization, a wild incitement of the poor and, according to the Talmud (*Sanhedrin 110a*), a vicious campaign of character assassination, in which Moses was accused of leading an immoral life. When Korah and his hordes ran out of arguments, they resorted to violence and tried to stone Moses.

Korah's rebellion failed. That result was inevitable because of its impure motives and corrupt methods. However, some of the ideas which the first anti-establishment rebellion articulated were to remain and bear fruit in later times.

Time for a Change

IT MUST HAVE been the worst news Moses ever heard: . . . "therefore you shall not bring this people into the land which I have given them" (*Numbers 20:12*). After spending a large part of a lifetime leading the Israelites out of bondage to their land, and enduring so much on their way, the leader is told that he will never reach the dreamt-of land. What heartbreak!

And what caused it all? Just one incident at a place called Me-Meribah, or waters of strife, in the Wilderness of Zin. What was the sin of Moses that deserved so severe a punishment?

Generations of Bible commentators tried to answer this question. The 19th-century scholar, S.D. Luzzato, after listing no less than thirteen different "sins" attributed to Moses that may have influenced God's judgment, concluded that he was not going to add another of his own to poor Moses, although all interpretations fell short of complying with the Biblical texts from which they derived. I am certainly not going to add another sin to the list, but rather try to put together a coherent picture from the various texts and commentaries.

There are many indications that Moses, the great and

experienced leader, had "lost his touch." The decision that he should step aside for a new leader was not a punishment, but rather the acknowledgement of a fact. Painful as it was, the prospect of Moses stepping aside had to be faced.

It all happened after the death of Miriam. This personal loss was a terrible blow to Moses. It was only then he must have realized how dependent he was on his big sister, the one who when he was still a baby had stood with a heavy heart on the river-bank, to make sure that her little brother would not drown. He had probably not realized till she died how much he needed, in his dealings with the people and the world, the support of his close family circle. They had been a natural trio—Miriam, Aaron, and Moses. Now it was no more.

Miriam died, and a perennial problem recurs in the form of a severe water shortage (*Numbers 20:1-2*). Moses, for the first time in his career, does not know how to deal with the crisis. Confronted by heated demonstrations, Moses retreats to his tent. He "falls on his face" (*ibid., 6*). Too unsure to face the people, he retreats from them into seclusion. The Lord orders him to "take the rod," to go back to the days of his youth, when with the rod in his hands he would rise to overcome many a crisis. He is to talk to the rock and bring forth water (*ibid., 8*). Moses, however, misunderstood the call. Instead of showing the strength of dignified leadership, his temper flares, and he insults the people: "hear now, ye rebels!" And in the same mood, he commits another mistake, an unforgivable one. Instead of *talking* to the rock, he *smites* it.

This is why the dreadful verdict has been pronounced: "You will not bring the people to the land." Moses, who began his career by admonishing the contentious Israelite

(*Exodus* 2:13): "Why do you smite your fellow?" has ended it by smiting a rock! Moses who knew how to face stormy situations in the past, now runs away and falls on his face. Moses, who set an example in how to treat his flock firmly but respectfully, now heaps insults on them. He could not be the leader anymore. He would not steer the people to the land.

Moses, we are told (*Numbers* 20:11), strikes the rock "*twice*". Any person can make a mistake once in an outburst of anger, but if he repeats his errors, he cannot be a leader. Aaron, who acted passively during this incident, is punished also and cannot enter the land. After the first striking of the rock Aaron could have pointed out to Moses his error and requested him to stop. When the rock was struck again, Aaron was in no position to claim "I didn't know." Through not protesting, he became an accomplice, and was penalized accordingly. Not only does Moses repeat his mistake, but Aaron's passivity is also duplicated—once at the incident of the rock, and once at the incident of the Golden Calf.

The Seven Books of Moses

AN OFT-QUOTED Talmudic tradition with regard to the canonization of the Bible (*Baba Bathra 14b*) includes the remarkable statement: "Moses set down in writing his own book, the Book of Balaam and the Book of Job." The fact that those two "books" were singled out from among all the books of the Bible to be attributed to Moses in addition to the five books of the Torah, the Pentateuch, has puzzled many a commentator, ancient and modern alike.

What the two stories of Balaam and Job have in common is that in both of them the protagonist is an outsider, a non-Jew. Thus, they help provide insight into the teachings of the Torah of Moses, which is the main body of Jewish law and belief. We may assume that some new perspectives of the laws of Moses are gained by the suggestion that none other than Moses penned the stories of Balaam and Job.

Job is the most tragic figure in biblical literature. He knew grief, bereavement, pain and disillusionment more than any other person in the Bible. The account of the vicissitudes, the inner struggles of such a person must therefore be the creation of the same man who set out to write down a Torah of eternal laws for human behavior.

Can one grasp the full meaning of the Law if one is cut off from human pain, aloof from human doubt and utter despair? In order that the laws of Moses should not become void of compassion for human beings, with all their painful shortcomings, Moses must be the man who is responsible for both his own book reflecting the law, and the book Job, reflecting life.

Rabbi Yitzhak Luria (1540–1572), known as the Ari Hakadosh ("Holy Lion"), and the greatest of Jewish mystics, spent his youth in Cairo. Every morning, at dawn, so the story goes, the Ari would stroll quietly among the reeds along the banks of the Nile.

"In order to delve into the real meaning of the laws of the Torah," he used to say, "I am trying to listen to the crying of the baby Moses who was thrown here among these reeds as a forlorn, helpless human being escaping persecution. Only one who can hear the cry of Moses the baby," concluded the Ari, "can properly grasp the words of Moses the law-giver."

When religious laws become divorced from the human situation they cease to be an expression of the will of God who cares.

Moses was constantly exhorting the Israelites to improve their behavior; he was overwhelmed by their rebellious moods and ungratefulness. In order for him to discover anew the greatness of his people, he had to hear it from the outside. In addition to his own book, he had to write the Book of Balaam.

Balak, the king of mighty Moab, was the first to realize—even before the Israelites recognized it themselves—that "a people has emerged out of Egypt." And Moab "was sore afraid." Balaam too was forced to sing the praises of Israel, as no other prophet, certainly not the prophets of Israel, ever did. He represents a proper counterbalance to the perspective of Moses, who was always reminding the Israelites of their faults.

Balak claimed that Balaam was very powerful in both blessings and curses (22:6). Why, then, did he not request the blessing of Balaam for his own people, rather than a curse on Israel? But, then as always, the enemies of Israel preferred its destruction, even at the expense of the destruction of their own peoples, to concentrating on constructive matters which would benefit both themselves and their neighbors.

Balaam came to curse and was forced eventually to turn his curses into blessings. It is worth noting that, to this day, Jewish daily prayer (as well as Israel Radio's daily broadcast) opens with the words of Balaam, the non-Jew: "How goodly are thy tents, O Jacob, thy dwellings, O Israel."

The basic and unique situation of Israel among the nations has not changed, however. In the phrase coined by Balaam (23:9), it is described as "a people which dwells alone." The same words became the title of a book by a contemporary Israeli diplomat (the late Dr. Yackov Herzog), describing the striking existential "aloneness" of Israel in the world arena of nations.

Choosing a Leader

THE MAIN CONCERN in the mind of Moses as he prepares to depart from this world is not his own family or private affairs. What occupies his mind most of all is his people. Worried about the appointment of a successor, he turns to God in prayer: "Let the Lord, the God of the spirits of all flesh, set a man over the congregation (*Numbers 27:16*)."

He presses for the appointment to take place *now*, not because he sees no proper candidate for the job. On the contrary, says the Rebbe of Kotzk, he does see a person who shows the qualities of a "natural" successor. This is Phinehas, who has just demonstrated a quality of leadership unmatched in courage and ingenuity by taking action in killing offenders and "turning the wrath of God" from his people.

The action of Phinehas the zealot was even endorsed by God himself. Yet, it is precisely this which frightens Moses, the experienced and trained leader. He likes Phinehas and no doubt approves of his valiant act, but at the same time he cannot see how this zealot, who in a moment of crisis decided to take the law into his own hands, can become the permanent leader of his people.

He asks God to name the new leader and goes on to specify the qualifications he would like to find in the
appointee.

According to Rashi, the classical commentator, and the
Midrash, the implicit meaning of Moses' prayer to God is
as follows:

"Sovereign of the universe, 'God of the spirits of all
flesh,' thou knowest the minds of all men, and how the
mind of one man differs from that of another. Appoint
over them a leader who will be able to bear with the dif-
fering spirits of every one of your children."

The true leader is not a single-minded fanatic, but a
person able to tolerate *all* views. "A man *over* the congregation," one who is above petty party politics.

When God responds to Moses' prayer, naming Joshua
as the future leader (*verse 18*), he describes him as "a man
in whom there is spirit." Here Rashi comments: "a man
who knows how to stand up *against* the spirit of each one
of them," to teach us that to be tolerant does not necessarily imply passivity or spinelessness. A good leader must
know his own mind, he must be able to stand up for his
views, he also must be capable of changing his mind, of
freeing himself from preconceived ideas. He must not be
the type who declares: "My mind is made up—don't con-
fuse me with facts."

Among the "signs" of deterioration which will occur
prior to the arrival of the Messiah, the Talmud mentions
pnei hador kifnei he-kelev (leaders with the character of a
dog).

Comments the Hafetz Hayim: A dog usually runs
ahead in front of his master, and it looks as if he is leading
the way. In fact, however, the dog stops from time to time
to look back and see in which direction the master wants

to go. A leader who keeps looking back to see where the masses want him to go, is no leader and is likened to a dog.

What other qualities, besides a firm and open mind, does Moses want to find in his successor? "A man that will go *before* them." An ancient midrash (*Sifrei*) interprets this in the following way: "Not like kings of other nations who send their troops into battle while they themselves stay behind, but someone who goes *before* his troops."

For many years, the pride of the Israel Defense Forces (IDF) and part of its "secret weapon" was the fact that the command to go into battle or any other dangerous operation, was not "Go!" but "*aharai*—Follow me!" The commander always going "before them."

Moses goes on asking that his successor be one "who may lead them out (to war) and who may bring them in." He knew well that it is one thing to take a people out *to* war and another to get them out *of* war and bring them back home. The second task is much harder. A true leader has to be capable of both.

And the Lord said to Moses: "Take thee Joshua the son of Nun." Joshua, we know, was Moses' closest aide for years. He was the "young man who departed not out of Moses' tent" (*Exodus 33:11*), and yet Moses did not think of him as his successor until told by God: Here is your man in your own back yard. "Lay thine hand on him."

Moses does what he is told and he does it wholeheartedly. Instead of laying one hand, he "laid both his hands upon him" (*Numbers 27:23*). Thus a leader was chosen and entrusted with the tremendous task of taking the people into their long-awaited Promised Land.

Sharing the Responsibility

AFTER A LONG sojourn in the desert, after going through so many trials and tribulations, the Children of Israel are now about to enter the Promised Land. They stand at the gate of the Land about which they dreamed so long and for which they suffered so much. They move towards their coveted destination with renewed strength and unity having several glorious military victories already behind them. The last thing one would expect at such a moment is a separatist move coming from two distinguished tribes. But that is exactly what happened when the tribes of Reuben and Gad approached Moses and expressed their desire to be permitted to stay in their lands which were recently conquered while *en route* to the Promised Land.

They appeal to Moses (*Numbers 32:5*): "Bring us not over the Jordan." They do not say openly that they want to separate themselves from the rest of Israel, who are heading towards the Land; all they want is to be exempted from the personal obligation of *aliya*.

The reason for this unexpected request lies in the fact which is told at the beginning of the story—that "the children of Reuben and the children of Gad had a great multitude of cattle." They had too much wealth invested in the country in which they lived now. They were too well-to-do to take *aliya* seriously.

In the plea of the tribesmen of Reuben and Gad to Moses, they used the most polite and humble language: "If we found *favor in thy sight,* let this land be given unto *thy servants* for a possession."

Not so Moses. In his answer, he bluntly and poignantly puts the challenge to them: "Shall your brethren go to the war and ye shall sit here?"

Those harsh words, perhaps among the most stern in the entire Bible, are echoed 1400 years later in a letter sent around the year 135 CE by Bar-Kokhba to the people of Ein-Gedi and unearthed a few years ago by the late Yigael Yadin. The letter, written on a papyrus size 9 x 19 centimeters, reads:

> From Shimeon bar Kosiba
> to the men of Ein-gedi
> to Masbala and to Yehonatan Bar-Beayan,
> Peace.
> In comfort you sit,
> eat and drink from the property of the
> House of Israel,
> and care nothing for your brothers.

The rest of the letter was not found, but Yadin remarked about it: "What a touching and a tragic note is in these words, written by the failing Prince of Israel . . . it is also perhaps the most indicative of Bar-Kokhba's desperate situation at the end of the revolt."

I recall, likewise, an exchange which took place at the Zionist Executive Committee meeting in Jerusalem during the grave days of the War of Liberation in 1948. The veteran American leader Rabbi Israel Goldstein declared at that time that the Jews of the United States and the

Jews of Israel were partners in the struggle for the Jewish state about to be established. The partnership—said Goldstein—is in the Hebrew word *damim*, which means both blood and money. We American Jews, he said, put our *damim*—money—into the partnership. You, Israeli Jews, give your *damim*—blood.

At this point, Rabbi Meir Bar-Ilan, the leader of the religious Zionists, rose to reply to Rabbi Goldstein: Indeed, he said, we are partners in the word *damim*, but what an immense difference between the two partners! When an Israeli Jew gives his blood for his people, he gives it to the last drop: Is there an American Jew who would give to his last dollar?

Moreover, when Israeli parents send their child into battle—it hurts them very much. Is there an American Jew who would give until it hurts? Oh yes, concluded Rabbi Bar-Ilan sarcastically, that happens. There are those who start hurting as soon as they give their first dollar!

We may assume that Moses was not so much concerned that the war would not be won if the tribesmen of Reuben and Gad did not take part in it; he believed that the Land would be conquered in accordance with God's promise, no matter how many tribes participated in it.

Moses's concern was, however, with the ethical implications of the seceding of the two tribes from a war which should be fought by all of Israel. The conquest of Eretz Yisrael was not encumbent only on those people who planned to live on the land. It was, in the eyes of Moses, the culmination of the drama of redemption which should be acted out in full by all the tribes that came out of Egypt.

Moses was likewise concerned with the effect that the step taken by Reuben and Gad might have on the morale of the people—"and therefore, will ye turn away the heart of the Children of Israel from going over into the Land which the Lord hath given them?"

He scolded them in sharp words, the likes of which he did not use even when they committed their gravest sins. "A brood of sinful men," he called them, recalling the sin committed against the Land by their "fathers," the slanderous spies.

Moses's sharp reprimand was not without results. When they returned, it was to tell him: "We will build sheepfolds here for our cattle and cities for our little ones, but we ourselves will be ready armed to go before the Children of Israel until we have brought them into our place. . . . We will not return unto our houses until the Children of Israel have inherited every man his inheritance."

Only on this condition did Moses agree that the tribes of Reuben and Gad take up settlement on the other side of the Jordan. It seems, that, in principle, he was not against Jews living outside the prescribed borders of the Land. He was, however, vehemently opposed to the unequal sharing among the tribes of Israel of the burden and responsibilities of the fight for the Land.

Once the tribesmen of Reuben and Gad offered to become *halutzim* (this is the term used in the Hebrew Bible, carried over to those early pioneers who settled Eretz Yisrael in recent generations) in the conquest of the Land alongside their brethren who were to settle there permanently, Moses considered them to be "clear before the Lord and before Israel."

A sin "before Israel" ranks in the eyes of Moses at the same level as a sin "before the Lord." Only when cleared from both sins, by the commitment to join the rest of Israel in its crucial struggles, do the people of Reuben and

Gad receive the Blessing of Moses to set themselves up with their children and rich possessions outside the Land of Israel.

Their full involvement in the life of the Land of Israel was the best guarantee for the safeguarding of Jewish wealth outside of Israel and certainly for the proper upbringing of Jewish children.

Facing Reality

"AND THE LORD spoke unto Moses, saying: Command the Children of Israel, and say unto them: When ye come into the land of Canaan, this is the land that shall fall unto you for an inheritance" (*Numbers 34:1-2*).

As they reach the end of the road, God wants to make sure that they know that "This is the land," this and none other.

No more promises of "milk and honey," no more threats of the "fierce people who dwell in the land" (*Numbers 13:28*), no more rumors of all kinds regarding the land. Now, on the day after they come out of the wilderness and into the land, they must start seeing reality as it is, with all its problems and all its potential blessings. "This is the land!"

The task of looking directly into the eyes of the real is not as easy as it sounds. This is particularly the case when it comes to relating to the land—most people would rather live with their preconceived ideas, than face changing realities which may demand of them to alter their previous personal orientations. If this attitude could be understood, even condoned, as long as one is still on the road

to the land—it is unforgivable and might spell havoc once
he enters the land to live there. At this point one is forced
to face reality as it is, and not to get lost in self-delusions.

I will always remember one of my first encounters with
Jews outside Israel which took place many years ago, in a
small town in Connecticut, U.S. It was on a visit to the
local Jewish day school. The principal of the school assembled his pupils—some sixty in number—to welcome
the guest from Israel. Showing off their Hebrew knowledge, which they must have diligently rehearsed in honor
of the occasion, the principal presented me to the assembly in Ashkenazi-accented Hebrew, saying, "*Ho-ish hozeh
hu oreiah me'eretz Yisroel,*" (this man is a guest from Israel).
As he said it, the children responded in chorus: "Sho-
lom!" The principal turning to the assembled children,
then continued with a question, "*Atem yod'im mi hai be-
eretz Yisroel?*" (Do you know who lives in the land of Israel?) To which all the children, again in sing-song chorus,
replied, "*Kein! Ho-halutzim hayim be'eretz Yisroel!*" (Yes, the
pioneers live in the land of Israel.)
    "*V'atem yod'im mah osim ho-halutzim ba-yom?*" (And do
you know what the pioneers do during the day?) And the
children replied, "*Kein, ho-halutzim ovdim es ho-odomo ba-
yom!*" (Yes, the pioneers till the land during the day.) "*U-
mah osim ho-halutzim ba-lailo?*" (And what do the pioneers
do at night?)
    To which the children replied "*Ho-halutzim rokdim hora
balailo!*" (The pioneers dance the *hora* at night.)
    I must confess, that it indeed felt wonderful to come
from a country where pioneers till the land during the
day, dance the hora at night and go out to fight for their
country in between the *minha* and *maariv* services at twi-
light. What was shocking, however, was the fact that not

only did some tots in a Connecticut Hebrew school live with a completely unrealistic picture of the land of Israel, but together with them were also many adults, some of them leaders of the community, some who had even visited Israel more than once.

Equally shocking in their escape from reality as those who see Israel as a paradise on earth are those who prefer a totally dark picture of Israel as an awful, corrupt, dismal, discriminatory place, a kind of hell on earth.

Unfortunately, both those who see only the bright side of the picture as well as those who see only its dark side commit the very same sin, refusing to heed the command of the Lord: "When thou come into the land . . . This is the land!" See it as it is. Only in that way can one render the land the best service without diminishing at all from the love for her.

"We expected to get from you inspiration—instead you gave us information," said the somewhat disappointed chairman of a meeting of teachers I addressed recently at the Bureau of Jewish Education in New York City. It was hard to convince him that inspiration which comes at the expense of information is futile and worthless. That is precisely what the Torah understood in regard to the land when we were warned, as we read the instructions given by Moses prior to entering the land (*Numbers 35:33*): "*Ve-lo tahanifu et ha-aretz,*" usually translated: "You shall not pollute the land," but which could also be translated correctly: "You shall not flatter the land." This is followed (*ibid.*, 34) with the warning: "*Ve-lo tetame et ha-aretz*"— "You shall not defile the land."

The proper attitude to the land requires that one does not "flatter" her and paint her with rosy colors, nor "defile" her and portray her as a dark monster, but that one knows, without fooling oneself that "this is the land," the land of Israel and the only Jewish State we have. This is the land, on the day after coming out of the wilderness, with all her shadows and lights of which there are plenty.

DEUTERONOMY   דברים

עֲלֵה רֹאשׁ הַפִּסְגָּה וְשָׂא עֵינֶיךָ
יָמָּה וְצָפֹנָה וְתֵימָנָה וּמִזְרָחָה וּרְאֵה
בְעֵינֶיךָ

Go up to the top of the Pisga, and
lift up thy eyes westward, and
northward, and southward, and
eastward, and behold with thy eyes:

Deuteronomy 3:27

A Time for Action, Another for Words

"THESE ARE THE WORDS which Moses spoke unto all Israel." Thus begins the fifth and concluding book of the Pentateuch. In the Hebrew Bible this book is called *Devarim* meaning, simply "words." The words referred to comprise the parting speech of Moses that covers, according to tradition, the entire book of Deuteronomy.

Moses appears in this book, from its placid, prosaic beginning to its stormy poetic end, as a most eloquent speaker. The opening verse of Deuteronomy serves to emphasize this fact: "*These* are the words which Moses spoke." The presentation of Moses as a man of words at this juncture in his life immediately brings to mind another turning point in the life of Moses.

Forty years earlier, the young shepherd Moses, a fugitive from the wrath of Pharaoh's police, experiences an extraordinary encounter in the desert. God speaks to him from the burning bush and commands him to go and bring the Children of Israel out of bondage. Moses replies *(Exodus 4:10):* "Oh, Lord. *I am not a man of words.*" This argument, as we know, was not accepted.

It is interesting, however, to see what happened to the very same Moses during the years that passed after that encounter in the desert. What turned someone who was "not a man of words" into a man of many words, capable of holding our rapt attention throughout an entire book of "words"?

Had Moses been a man of words when he first assumed the mission of freeing the Israelites from Egypt, he might have become, as so often happens, a captive of his own eloquence. He might have spent the rest of his life making fiery speeches and expending his energies on flowery slogans about the supreme importance of liberation and freedom. What was needed at that time in the life of the people of Israel was a man of action, not words.

Only many years later, with a glorious record of action behind him, does Moses become a man of words, words of teaching and rebuke. At this point in the liberation process, he considered these no less vital to the fulfillment of the dream of freedom than the actions of the past.

This point seems to be stressed in the biblical narration: "These are the words which Moses spoke . . . *after* he had smitten Sihon the King of Heshbon" (*Deuteronomy 1:1–4*). If Moses can now speak freely about the wars which the people are to face in order to enter the land which lies ahead of them, it is only because he himself has personally participated in war.

Moses realizes that only a leader who had risked his own life and brought much good to his people has the right to rebuke them for their shortcomings. He must have wanted to say these "words" earlier, but he waited for the right moment. That is why the biblical narrative puts so much emphasis on the place and time of Moses's speech.

That right moment came not only after he had scored spectacular victories on the battlefield, but also after he had transferred the helm of leadership to Joshua and thus could not be suspected of having some personal axe to grind.

This portion of the Bible is always read in the synagogue on the Sabbath prior to the 9th of Av, the day of mourning which commemorates the destruction of the Temple and the loss of Jewish independence.

The rabbis point out that there is one word which connects the Sabbath Torah reading to the book of Lamentations, mandatory for the 9th of Av. The word is *eicha*, ("how"), which features prominently both in the words of Moses *(Deuteronomy 1:12)* and in the opening of Lamentations: "*How* does the city sit solitary, that was full of people?"

"How" and not "why" is the word with which the Bible confronts catastrophe and evil. We are not to look weepingly at calamity and cry, "Why did it happen to me?" We may never find out. What is important, however, is to investigate how the evil occurred. It may help us avoid it next time. Also, now that it has happened, how are we to cope with it? How are we to combat calamity; how are we to overcome and eradicate evil?

Both Moses and Jeremiah, at different crucial stages in the life of Israel, boldly asked, "How?"

Knowing "how" it happened, how things deteriorated gradually until they reached the present low stage, may help us also find the answer to the question of "why" they happened the way they happened.

First Refusenik

"AND I BESOUGHT the Lord at that time saying: O Lord God, thou hast begun to show thy servant thy greatness and thy strong hand. . . . Let me go over, I pray thee, and see the good land that is beyond the Jordan, that goodly mountain and Lebanon" *(Deuteronomy 3:23–25)*.

According to the rabbis, this is only the essence of Moses' plea to gain entrance into the Land. In reality, he used countless arguments to justify and substantiate his request. Despite this he was denied entrance to the Land. Thus, Moses was the first "refusenik," and it seems that since then there have always been those who can go to the Land, but do not want to, and those who desperately want to, but are not able to do so.

Of course, the analogy between Moses and modern-day "refuseniks" should not be stretched too far; what they obviously do have in common, however, is the heartbreak and deep frustration caused by the refusal to allow them to fulfill their life's dream—to enter the Land.

The sages in the Midrash read much into this situation. They try to visualize how Moses must have felt at that moment, and accordingly they elaborate on the words

which Moses used when he spoke to God, and the arguments he employed. They also bring the counter-
arguments used by God to convince Moses, His beloved
messenger, that the leader had to die at this juncture and
thus clear the way for a different type of leadership required for the people as they leave their nomadic desert
life and proceed to the next stage: conquest and settlement of the Land.

According to the Midrash, Moses begins his long but
futile plea by saying, "Lord of the Universe, consider how
much I had to bear for the sake of Israel, until they became 'Thy claim and Thy possession.' I suffered with
them so much, shall I not take part in their rejoicing?"

Demanding justice, Moses bases his claims on God's
own Torah. "Look Thou," he argues: "By forbidding me
to enter the Promised Land, Thou givest the lie to Thy
Torah, for it says, 'In his day thou shalt give the laborer
his hire.' Where then is my hire for the forty years during
which I labored for the sake of Thy children and for their
sake suffered much sorrow. . . ."

Moses also resorts to evoking compassion for himself as
a retired veteran servant of his people. "All the time that
we were in the desert," he pleads, "I could not sit quietly
even for one moment just to study and enjoy life. Look at
all the books I was planning to read and write, all the
things I had in mind to do when entering the Holy Land,
and now you are telling me that my time is up?" Moses,
the man of God, the obedient servant, contrary to all
expectations—refuses to take it lying down.

He makes every effort to postpone, if not to cancel altogether, the summons to join his ancestors. The main reason for this is his burning desire to go up to "The Land," if
not as a permanent settler, at least to visit it as a tourist.
"Let me go over and *see* the good land."

The same sentiment is expressed in a beautiful, yet little known Hassidic story. The saintly Baal-Shem-Tov, the story goes, accended to heaven. After spending some time there, he was offered the rare privilege of staying there permanently, thus being spared the agonies of death. The Baal-Shem-Tov rejoiced at the offer, but after some reflection, refused to accept it—because that would deprive him of fulfilling the hope he still nurtured of going to Eretz Israel. (That he actually harbored such hope is clear from the only authentic letter we have from the Baal-Shem-Tov, the famous *Igeret Hakodesh*.)

Notwithstanding all of Moses' arguments, God did not change His verdict. Every generation, He told Moses, must have its own leaders. Moses must remain where his own generation is buried. The shepherd must stay with his flock. Not even his remains can be brought to the land of his dreams. When Moses questions why he is worse than Joseph, whose bones will enter the Land, he receives a scathing answer: Joseph, unlike Moses, when confronting the outside world, was proud of belonging to his people and his land, therefore he merits the privilege of being buried there.

Where do we know that Joseph acknowledged the Land, while Moses failed to do so? The rabbis (in *Devarim Rabbah 2:8*) quote the story in Genesis *(39:14)*, when his mistress exclaimed, "See! he has brought a Hebrew . . ." and he, Joseph, did not deny it. Moreover Joseph, when talking about himself *(Genesis 40:15)* affirms, "For indeed, I was stolen away from the land of the Hebrews."

On the other hand, Moses keeps quiet when the daughters of Jethro *(Exodus 2:19)* say, "An Egyptian prince delivered us out of the hands of the shepherds." He does not correct them to say he is a Hebrew. And he does not seem to object to appearing in the eyes of the young ladies as a good WESP (Worthy Egyptian Saving Prince) not rushing to make known to them the truth of his being a Hebrew.

This seemingly minor incident is taken into account when his application to enter the land is considered. One cannot cover up one's national identity at a moment of convenience and at the same time expect to be rewarded a full share in the national celebration after the destination is reached. Even if one is none other than Moses, the redeemer of Israel, himself.

The Strangers

"FOR THE LORD your God, he is God of Gods, and the Lord of Lords, the great God, the mighty and the awful, who regardeth not persons, or takes reward." Against this awesome and emphasized greatness, a reminder: "He does execute justice for the fatherless and widow, and loves the stranger, in giving him food and raiment." As great and mighty as he is, he is not too great or too preoccupied to deal directly with the small man in the street, even with the rejects and marginals of society. He also asks the same of us: "Love ye therefore the stranger, for ye were strangers in the land of Egypt" (*Deuteronomy 10:17–19*).

According to the Talmud (*Baba Metzia 59b*) the injunction to love the stranger and treat him in justice and mercy appears no less than thirty-six, some say forty-six, times in the Bible. The fact that it is reiterated so many times tells us two things: first, that it must be of utmost importance in the eyes of the Bible; secondly, that it is most probably a neglected area, or something which people are liable to forget, to overlook, or even find all kinds of "explanations" to do away with. The Torah repeats again and again: Remember, you must not mistreat the stranger within thy gates, nor can you evade the issue.

The reason usually accorded in the Bible for the special awareness which we are to cultivate towards strangers is "because you yourselves were strangers in the land of Egypt." In which way does the fact that a person has himself suffered oblige him to consider others who are in a similar situation? On the contrary, we know that sometimes there is a reverse effect to suffering. It hardens one and makes him insensitive to the suffering of others.

There is also the element of the "slave become king" who is among the most despicable of characters in the Bible *(Proverbs 30:22)* as well as in human life. Why is it, then, that almost every time the Torah warns us regarding the treatment of strangers—it reminds us that we too were strangers?

Jewish commentators throughout the ages offer different answers to this question. Let us look at some of them.

In a way, the Bible itself in several places offers further insight into this reason of our being strangers for the way we must treat other strangers. Take, for instance, Exodus 23:9: "And a stranger shalt thou not oppress, for ye know the heart of a stranger, seeing you were strangers in Egypt." Here, when dealing with the warning against oppressing, or simply, putting pressure on the stranger, the Torah adds to the usual rationale "because you were strangers," also the words "for you know the heart of the stranger."

One is expected to demonstrate compassion towards the stranger, out of empathy which stems from one's own personal experience. Rashi (Rabbi Shlomo Itzhaki, 1040–1105), the classical commentator of the Torah, adds in his usual laconic but mild way: "You know the heart of the stranger—you know how hard it is for him when he is being pressed." One is not allowed, of course, to oppress or put pressure on anyone, but from one's past experience one should know how hard it is for the stranger when he is excessively pressed. What may be "normal" to other people, appears oppressive and painful to the stranger. It is not enough to treat the stranger in the same way as other citizens; one must bend over backwards, and show particular consideration for the stranger, because he is particularly sensitive and prone to be hurt.

Abraham Ibn Ezra (1093–1167), the famous medieval poet and Bible commentator, points to the fact that the stranger usually appears in the company of the widow and the orphan, as we are warned against mistreating all helpless, defenseless and voiceless elements in the society. These people often find themselves in a position where they cry for help—but there is no one there to hear them. Yet, this seems so only to the outside onlooker; in fact, their voice is not lost. "For if you afflict them, if they cry unto me, I will surely hear their voice" *(Exodus 22:22).*

It is a mistake to think that those distressed people are alone, that their cry is lost. They are not alone for God is with them. He also hears and responds to their cry. This is substantiated in the lines: "You were strangers in the land of Egypt" and look, you were not lost, because God heard you and saved you. So, beware of the way you treat the stranger, because his cry is heard, as was yours.

Ibn Ezra furthermore points to the stylistic change in the mistreatment of the powerless in Exodus *(22:20–22)* from the singular to the plural. It is to tell us that if one witnesses the oppression of the stranger or the poor, or knows of it, and keeps quiet about it, one becomes by one's silence an accomplice to the crime, even though having no active part in it. This person too will be punished along with the oppressors. Ibn Ezra is more extreme on this issue than the famous activist Rabbi Abraham Joshua Heschel, when he said that "in a free society, some are guilty—all are responsible."

Nachmanides (Ramban—Rabbi Moshe Ben Nachman,

1194–1270) carries this point further to explain the rationale of "because you were strangers in the land of Egypt." Why, says Ramban, does one think that he might discriminate against the stranger and oppress him? Because he feels that he is in command of power which the stranger does not possess. The Torah reminds us that in our history we saw more than once how the wheel could turn. The one who is powerless now could very easily get to power. Proof of this is that "you were strangers in the land of Egypt," and look at you now. It is, therefore, not only kind and noble to treat the stranger with justice, it is also desirable out of sheer pragmatic expediency.

The proper treatment of the stranger which the Bible requires of us does not remain in the realm of lofty ideals paying lip-service to human rights in general. It is spelled out over and over again, in concrete terms. It must be expressed in equality in law and justice (*Leviticus 24:22*), in equal working conditions and equal pay for labor (*Deuteronomy 24:14*), an equal share in welfare support (*Leviticus 25:35*), and above all in respect and love. This last requirement, love, being the hardest, is repeated several times, and reaches its peak in the Code of Holiness (*Leviticus 19:33*): "And if a stranger sojourns with you in your land, you shall not do him wrong. The stranger . . . shall be unto you as the home-born among you, and you shall love him as thyself; for you were strangers in the land of Egypt. I am the Lord your God."

"Love him like yourself" could very well mean, love him because *he is* like yourself. He is a human being with feelings and emotions and the right to live with you in dignity. The conclusive close, "I am the Lord your God" is said in the plural: *ani hashem elohi-khem*. Why? Rashi says: I am *your* God. I am as well *his* God. And Heschel said: "God is either the father of all man, or of no man."

The Art of Giving

THE BOOK OF Deuteronomy (*Deutro nomos*, a translation of the Hebrew *Mishne Torah*), meaning second law, deals primarily with the presentation of a blue-print for the life of an ideal society coming into its promised land. It prescribes every detail of the good life, which not only makes a people prosperous and happy, but also grants every individual the status of full equality in the eyes of the law and in the range of opportunities open to each.

An ideal, if not a Utopian picture, is described in the unfolding chapters of Deuteronomy, yet it is realistic enough to accept the sober fact that "poor folk will never cease to be in the land" *(Deuteronomy 15:11)*. Human society, even at the peak of its social advancement, will always have its deprived and its poor. Their immediate problems should not be "tabled" until such a time when the overall reform of the "system" will take place, but it is you, as an individual, that "I command to open *your* hand to *your* fellows, to the destitute and the needy in *your* land" *(ibid., 11)*.

This command of an "open hand" for charity, uttered by Moses in the wilderness, accompanied Israel throughout its history, playing a most important role in the dramatic survival of the Jewish people and remains today a typical trait—almost second nature—of the individual Jew.

A few years ago, on a visit to America, I was told the amusing story about an army corporal at morning parade calling off the names of the men in his unit:

"Kelly!" he shouted.

"Here," came the response.

"Armstrong!"

"Here."

Then came the turn of Private Cohen.

"Cohen!" shouted the corporal. Whereupon Cohen, being accustomed to so many charity appeals, automatically responded:

"Twenty-five dollars!"

Private Cohen's response was undoubtedly an echo of the words expressed thousands of years earlier, and since then ingrained over so many generations into the Jewish way of life; "If you have a poor man of your fellow countrymen, in any township of the land which the Eternal your God gives you, you must not harden your heart, nor shut your hand, against your poor brother. You must open your hand to him, lending enough to meet his needs" (*15:7–8*).

Like most other commandments in the Torah, this command too did not remain a piece of moralistic advice, but has been embodied in a set of laws which prescribes, in great detail, *when* and *how* a person should put into practice this "open hand" policy.

Moses says, "If you have a poor man of your fellow countrymen," and the Rabbis from here derived the rule that "The poor of thine own city should be helped before those of another city" (*TB Baba Metzia 71a*).

Moses also says, "In any township which the Eternal gives you," derive from the Rabbis this, that one must assist the poor in the Holy Land, before helping anyone who dwells outside the land of Israel.

All the laws of giving are grouped under the heading of tzedaka, translated usually as charity, but actually meaning righteousness.

The Rabbis' choice of the term *tzedaka* for the act of helping the poor could not have been accidental; it is in effect the theory that assisting the poor is not an act of grace on the part of the donor, but a duty. By giving charity the donor is merely practicing righteousness—performing a deed of justice. As such, no less important than the giving itself is the "art of giving." The Torah warns us *(Deuteronomy 15:10)* "you should surely give . . . (but) your heart should not grieve when you give."

Opening our hand to the needy should not be tainted by committing them to go through a maze of committees and networks of social workers and bureaucrats, who sometimes forget that their job is to offer help and alleviate distress. The Torah expects that we teach ourselves how to give "with a smile," and not grieve and complain while giving of financial difficulties, and the like.

Maimondides (1135–1204), the great codifier of Jewish Law, states this principle in clear terms, "Whoever closes his eyes against charity is, like the idol-worshipper, impious . . . whoever gives alms to the poor with bad grace and downcast looks, though he bestow a thousand gold pieces, all the merit of his action is lost; but he must give with grace, gladly, sympathizing with the poor man in distress." Maimonides also suggests the structure of the following eight-stage ladder in the art of giving, each stage lower than the other, until we reach the lowest stage.

Better than helping the poor in giving charity is granting the needy a gift of a loan, entering into a partnership with him or procuring him work, thereby helping him to become self-supporting. Inferior to this is giving charity in such a way that the giver and the recipient are unknown to each other; next is the donation of money to a charitable fund of the community; below this is the instance where the donor is aware of to whom he is giving charity, but the recipient is unaware of from whom he received it; next is the case where the recipient knows the identity of the donor but not *vice versa* (like the Rabbis about whom it is told in the Talmud, Ketubot, 67b, that they used to tie sums of money in linen bundles and throw them behind their backs for the poor people to pick up, so that they should not feel shame).

The next four degrees are: one who gives money to the poor before he is asked; one who gives money to the poor after he is asked; one who gives less than he should; but does it with good grace, and lastly, at the very bottom of the ladder, he who gives grudgingly (*Yad. Matnot Ani'im, 10:1–14*).

The sages of the Talmud (*Baba Bathra 9a*) considered "charity equal to all other precepts put together" and Maimonides, in the twelfth century, after setting forth in detail all the laws pertaining to *tzedaka*, testifies that "we have never heard or seen a Jewish community without a charity chest."

The Pursuit of Justice

THE MORE translations one reads of the Bible, the more convinced one becomes that there is no way of getting the real flavor of the biblical text without resorting to the original Hebrew. When comparing the original text with its translations, even the best of them, one is reminded of David Ben-Gurion, who is reputed to have said that reading the Bible in translation is like kissing your beloved through a handkerchief.

The latest translation of the Bible is that published by the Jewish Publication Society. While the King James version reads *(Deuteronomy 16:18)*, "Judges and officers shalt thou make thee in all the gates which the Lord your God gives thee throughout thy tribes," the new Jewish Publication Society translation reads, "You shall appoint magistrates and officials for your tribes, in all the settlements that the Lord your God is giving you."

While the latter translation is not incorrect, it loses some of the ideas that may be attached to the Hebrew text. For example, when told to appoint judges, the Scripture uses the word *lekha*, translated by King James as "shalt thou make thee"; in the New English Bible it translates as "you shall appoint for yourselves."

This was left out of the JPS translation, probably for the sake of brevity and clarity. It thereby loses however a beautiful comment derived from a clue in the word *lekha*— namely, that prior to judging others, one must first judge oneself. "Make thee," or "appoint for yourselves" first, and only then may you have the moral right to judge others.

The Midrash tells the following story: Rabbi Hanina ben Elazar had a tree in his field, the branches of which spread out into someone else's field. One day, a man came to Rabbi Hanina's court, requesting his neighbor to remove the branches of a tree that reached into his field. Rabbi Hanina told the claimant to return the following day. When the man complained, "You always pass judgment on the same day, why do you make me wait another day," Rabbi Hanina did not answer.

As soon as the man left, Rabbi Hanina sent workers to cut down the branches from his own tree that were falling into the field of his neighbor. The next day, when the complainant came back and his neighbor was ordered by Rabbi Hanina to cut off the branches of his tree, the man protested: "Why, you yourself have a tree with branches falling into someone else's area!" And Rabbi Hanina answered calmly, "You are right, please go out to my field, and make sure to keep yours the same way mine is kept."

If one does not judge oneself first, how can one judge others?

Torah orders the appointment of "judges and officers", as one without the other is not sufficient. As beautified as a law may be, if it does not possess "teeth", if there are no law enforcing officers, the law and the verdict based upon it are utterly worthless. Nor should the law be taken into anyone's hands without the proper procedure of the judiciary.

Let us take one more example: following the order to appoint judges that will not pervert the cause of justice, the Torah again warns us *(verse 20)* "Justice, justice shalt thou pursue" or "follow." The question is obvious: why is the word justice, *zedek*, repeated?

The Revised Authorized translation renders it this way, "That which is altogether just, shalt thou follow," while the New English Bible reads, "justice, and justice alone." If we stay however with the original Hebrew, the repetition of the word *zedek* may come to teach us that it is important not only to pursue justice, as one of the highest ideals of Judaism, but that also this pursuit must be carried out in just ways. "Justice (in) Justice (in just ways) shall you pursue." The end in no way justifies the means.

Furthermore, "justice" is cited twice to teach us yet another lesson, that when pursuing justice we cannot remain one-sided.

While there are those who perceive justice to be always on their side, there are others, who in their fervor to do justice to their opponents, tend to forget that there is justice also on their own side.

It is, indeed, much more difficult to find a way between two claims, both of whom have justice on their side, than to decide *a priori* which of the two sides is absolutely just and must be aided.

That is why the Torah twice uses the word justice, "justice, justice—(both sides of justice)—shall you pursue, that thou mayest live and inherit the land."

Generation Gap

THE COMPLAINT sounds familiar. In the simple words of the Torah *(Deuteronomy 21:18–21)*: "If a man has a stubborn and rebellious son, who will not obey his father or his mother, who will not listen to them, even when they chastise him . . ." The Torah does not specify in which way the son will not obey. It does not state whether the son expresses his disobedience by demonstrating in the streets, being seen in bad company, taking drugs, or simply escaping responsibility for his own life. Neither does the Torah mention what arguments this "stubborn and rebellious son" uses to explain disobeying his parents. We must assume, however, that this stubborn and rebellious son does not merely sit back silently. Youth is usually vocal and this child too must have a thing or two to say regarding his disenchantment with his parents' world, their way of thinking and acting, which lead him to disobey their will and way of life.

The case of the stubborn and rebellious son is preceded in the Torah by another case, that of "A man who has two wives, one of whom he loves and one of whom he slights, and both have borne him children." This case follows that of the soldier in battle taking prisoners of war and finding among the prisoners "a beautiful woman whom he desires and longs to marry."

Thus, some early commentators of the Bible saw in the sequel of cases a certain socio-psychological chain reaction. When out of sheer lust, a man marries the wrong woman, the result is a broken home, where both love and hate exist. Such a home devoid of real love is bound to produce that "stubborn and rebellious son."

The remedy the Torah offers for the problem of the generation gap is quite severe, with the parents denouncing their son to the elders of the town, "This son of ours is stubborn and rebellious, he does not hearken to our voice; he is a glutton and a drunkard." Following the parents' public indictment, "all the men of the city shall stone him to death. So shall you eradicate evil from you and all Israel shall hear and fear."

This radical solution to the problem of a stubborn and rebellious son did not seem likely even in the eyes of the rabbis in the Mishna and the Talmud. Thus, the second century scholar Rabbi Shimon boldly states: "The case of the stubborn and rebellious son being executed never occurred, neither will it ever occur."(Sanhedrin 71a).

The rabbis find it hard to accept that a son could be solely responsible for what he became. A stubborn and rebellious generation must be the backlash of certain attitudes of the society in which it was nurtured. Thus, when threshing, as they do, every single word of the scriptural text of the case under consideration, the rabbis come up with a series of limitations as to when and how parents can justly blame their son in public, demanding his punishment.

Rabbi Judah says (Mishna Sanhedrin 8:4): "If his mother was not fit for his father he cannot be blamed as a stubborn and rebellious son. If either one of them (father or mother) was maimed in the hand, or lame or dumb or blind or deaf, he cannot be condemned as a stubborn and rebellious son; for it is written 'then his father and mother shall lay hands upon him'—they cannot therefore be maimed in the hand; 'and bring him'—they cannot therefore be lame;" and so on.

Furthermore, in the Babylonian Talmud *(Sanhedrin p. 71a)* the list of limitations on the possible condemnation of the rebellious son grows: "If his mother did not resemble his father in voice, looks and size—the son cannot be condemned."

All these restrictions make it virtually impossible to execute a rebellious son by stoning him at any given time. The case put forward in the Torah serves, however, as a warning to remind us of the failures of the over-30 generation who inevitably produce a rebellious son.

Such a son is not to blame if the parents are "maimed," and do not raise a finger to do something in order to change the environment in which their child grows up. The son is not to blame if the parents are "lame" and cannot go out of their way to give up any of their own comforts in order to prevent results which they will later lament. The son is not to blame if the parents are "dumb" or "blind"—if they overlook or disregard the problems which young people face and cannot raise a voice to change the situation while this is still possible. Finally, the son is not entirely to blame for the morass into which he has landed, if the parents were "deaf" and could not or would not listen to the voice of the young, ignoring their outcry for more love, more understanding and more decent consideration.

The rebellious son can be blamed and punished only in a situation where there is full accord and harmony between father and mother in "voice, looks, and size," meaning when each one of the parents does not talk to the child in a voice different from the other, when they share a common outlook, and similarly size up the society in which their son is to grow up. In view of this, it is possible to understand why the rabbis state "that the execution of the rebellious son by stoning never occurred, never will occur."

The Gift of Joy

A GREAT NUMBER of the people mentioned in the Bible engage in prayer. Their prayers are almost without exception spontaneous and have grown out of a given situation. There are very few formulated prayers in the Bible. One is the set form of a prayer, also known in tradition as a "confession," to be recited at the offering of the first fruit. The exact words of the "confession," or statement, to be made on this occasion is fully prescribed in the Torah *(Deuteronomy 26:1–11)*.

"And it shall be, when thou art come in the land which the Lord, thy God, gives thee for an inheritance, and you possess it and dwellest therein; thou shalt take of all the first fruit of the earth . . . and thou shalt go up unto the priest and say unto him: I profess this day unto the Lord thy God that I am come to the country which the Lord swore unto our fathers to give us."

This is followed by a recounting of the highlights of the history of Israel, starting with our father who was a "wandering Aramean," until we reached this land after being liberated from bondage in Egypt.

This same statement also serves as the core of the Pessah night liturgy, the Haggada, comprising the tale of a

225

people on their way to freedom. The fact that the rabbis ordained the use of one and the same text for the two events comes to tell us that only then can freedom be fully manifested, when one can point to the actual first fruit that has resulted from the long process of liberation. Only when the fruit is in front of you can you unequivocally state: "I profess this day, that I am come to the country."

Only today is history, which at times seemed sad and senseless, redeemed. Thanksgiving for the land "which the Lord gives thee," was not possible until now, when this given land also witnessed the process of "you possess it and dwellest therein." The first fruit is concrete proof that this actually took place. The gift of God and the toil of humans combined in producing the fruit of the land, a token of freedom and a good reason for rejoicing.

Joy is something that comes spontaneously when one lives to see the first fruit of one's labor. Why then be ordered in the Torah *(verse 11)*: "And you should rejoice with all the good that the Lord your God gave you?" It is because far too often we are not ready to rejoice when good comes to us, as much as we are ready to complain and lament when the reverse happens.

It is indeed a special gift of God to be able to rejoice over the good. There are those who claim that it is raining when being spit at; on the other hand those who cry "spit" even when it is raining. Both types do not befit a free person, who has just begun to build a new healthy society in the new land. "Rejoice with all the good." Give thanks for every drop of blessing as it comes your way.

As the declaration to be made when offering the new fruit was set forth in its exact wording, the rabbis in subsequent generations tried to read particular meaning into each and every word of it. For example, they derive from the text that only a person who personally owns a piece of land is entitled to recite the statement in thanksgiving for the first fruit, as this would be impossible to come by without the land.

They also ruled in the Mishna (the first code of oral Jewish law, circa 200 CE), that a proselyte may partake in the new fruit offering, but cannot recite the text of the declaration, as it reads "the country which the Lord swore to our fathers" who, of course, were not the ancestors of the proselyte.

This ruling which must have been embarrassing to the proselyte, was reversed by the great medieval codifier of Jewish law Maimonides, who ruled in his Mishne Torah *(Bikurim 4:3)* that a proselyte, just like any Israelite, has to offer the first fruit and recite the full text of the declaration. As there is no other case where Maimonides would go against the ruling of the Mishna, this exceptional case was much discussed in the world of Jewish learning, until some decades ago when a hitherto unknown letter by Maimonides was discovered and published.

In this letter, which has often been quoted since then, Maimonides addresses himself to a proselyte, a former Arab by the name of Abdul-Alla, now Obadia (both names mean servant of the Lord) who painfully turned to Maimonides asking, how he, a descendent of pagans, could utter without lying the prayers which include the clause "Our God and God of our parents," knowing well that the God of Israel was not the God of his ancestors.

Maimonides, in his response, instructed him to recite all prayers as they are written, since Abraham himself was a proselyte, who converted from idolatry to the true ways of God, and in a sense Abraham's descendants are all who follow his ways, and all the proselytes. By embracing

Judaism, Maimonides reassures Obadiah, "Abraham is also your father, in no respect is there a difference between one who was born Jewish and you."

That is to say, that Judaism is not only perpetuated by race but also by faith, and conversely when one joins Judaism he not only joins a religious belief, but the history of a people. This point was brought out as well by Ruth, the prototype of the convert. As she is about to join the religion of her mother-in-law Naomi, she says "Your people will be my people," even before she says, "and your God will be my God" *(Ruth 1:16)*. By joining the Jewish religion, the convert joins the Jewish people and its history. Abraham, Isaac and Jacob, to whom the land was promised, are also ancestors of the proselyte. He can rightly say, therefore, the full text of the first fruit offering.

This view of Maimonides, running contrary to the Mishna, is supported by the opinion of Rabbi Judah as quoted in the Jerusalem Talmud *(Bikurim, 1:4)* interpreting the verse *(Genesis 17:5)* in which God says to Abraham "I have made you a father of a multitude of nations" to include Abraham's parenthood of gentiles who accept the faith and people of Abraham.

Choosing Life

MOSES REPEATEDLY PLEADS with the people that the one and only way of survival is to accept God's commandments as given in the Torah. He gives a full, detailed account of the blessings they shall receive as a result of "listening," and the curses which will befall them should they not listen.

He calls upon heaven and earth to be witnesses to the fact that he has actually laid down before the people, in no uncertain terms, the conditions for life and death, while he continues to plead, "Please, please choose life, that thou mayest live, thou and thy seed" *(Deuteronomy 30:19)*.

One might ask in the words of Erich Fromm: how can a human make a choice between life and death—except if one were to consider the possibility of suicide. What the biblical text refers to, says Fromm, is not life and death as biological facts, but as principals and values.

Being alive means growing, responding, developing. To be dead (even if biologically one is alive) means to stop growing, to fossilize, to become a lifeless object. Many people never face the clear alternative between the values of life and death, and thus living in neither world become "zombies," their bodies being alive and their souls dead. To choose life is the necessary condition for love, freedom, and truth. It is also the condition for loving God, for "not those who are dead praise the Lord," as the psalmist says.

"This person," as Reb Nahum of Chernobyl used to refer to one of his colleagues, "is already dead five years, yet no one bothered to tell him."

Furthermore, Moses is implying here that when the choice is made, one is to make sure that it is not for oneself alone, but for one's children as well. It is as if Moses were saying: Make sure that the way of the Torah you are accepting is not a way which creates a gap between the generations. A culture and a way of life cannot be tested in one generation. It stands the test only it if is perpetuated and proves viable for "you and your children."

The commandments prescribed in the Torah were meant to forge a link between parents and children, not to cause a rift between them. It is through the fulfillment of the commandments that families may come together to sit around the same table and share ideas and ideals.

Moses further tries to prove this point by defining the scope of Torah, "For this commandment which I command you this day is not too hard for thee, neither is it too far off" (*ibid., 11*). I am not talking to you (he says to the people) about a Utopia. I am not selling you a far-off idea, a visionary blue-print for a remote future. "It is not a heaven . . . Neither is it beyond the sea" (*ibid., 12–13*).

Some people may be under the impression that Torah is to be followed only by those people who live a heavenly life, who are extremely devout and removed from everyday realities of life. To them Moses says: "It is not in heaven!" The commandments are meant for earthly and healthy people, who are not overly steeped in heavenly pursuits, but go about their normal day-to-day life.

The Torah is as good for "earthly" Tel Aviv as it is for "heavenly" Jerusalem. "It is not in Heaven." "Neither is it beyond the sea." There are those who do admit that the prescribed way of life of the Torah is necessary for Jews abroad—that it is there that one has to be concerned about assimilation or disintegration. They are intensely concerned about the state of Jewish education in the United States, or disturbed about the closure of synagogues in the Soviet Union. However, the same people will not do anything concerning the fate of education for Judaism in their own neighborhood nor about the fact that they have not seen the inside of a synagogue for years. It is to these people that Moses cries out "neither is it beyond the sea." Torah is not only for those overseas.

The way of Judaism and Torah is not "far off," it is neither "in heaven," nor "beyond the sea." It is here and now. "The word is nigh unto thee, in thy mouth, and in thy heart, that thou mayest do it" (*ibid., 14*). Indeed, many may be ready to have the word of God in their mouths to give it lip-service at conventions and public meetings. Many may even claim that it is well to be "good Jews in heart." Both are no doubt performing a good service for Judaism. Yet, in the final analysis, both the "mouth Jews" and the "heart Jews" are not enough. The real purpose of the Torah is "that thou mayest do it."

It is the doing, the action, that assures the continuity of life.

Strong and of Good Courage

THERE WAS NO room left for shocks or surprises as to Moses' imminent death. God made it clear to Moses that he must not enter the Land and that the helm of leadership would pass on to his successor. Moses too, after much agonized pleading, complied with the will of the Almighty. He began preparing his people for the inevitable, addressing them in a long parting speech, which now makes up the bulk of the book of *devarim* ("words," or Deuteronomy).

In order to secure continuity and a peaceful transition of leadership, and to avoid a power struggle, Moses, following the advice of the Lord, chose Joshua as his successor. He presented Joshua in a public ceremony to the priesthood and the entire congregation, and laid both hands on him (*Numbers 27:15-23*). Yet, the difficult moment of the actual parting and transfer of power was still to come.

How would Moses feel and act at that moment? How would the people react? After more than forty years with Moses, sharing with him so many memorable occasions of exultation, trial, and tribulation, would it be possible for them to accept now his young assistant as their new

leader? And Joshua himself, having been accustomed for
many years to being second, or even third (after the high
priest) in command, would he be ready to step out from
behind the curtain into the full limelight of the leading
position? Would he be ready to assume full control at this
crucial moment in the life of his people, as they were
about to reach their destination? Would he not be awed by
the tremendous responsibility inherent in assuming a
command upon which would rest the fate of both the future and the past of his people, and in a way the destiny
of the world? If he failed, everything—all the achievements of Israel up to that point, the Exodus, the revelation
at Sinai, the shaping of the nation—all these would be
undone.

It is one thing to reach a theoretical understanding of
filling the office of his great and revered master, but the
actual takeover which was now at hand was an altogether
different challenge.

"And Moses went and spoke these words unto all Israel. And he said unto them: 'I am a hundred and twenty
years old this day; I can no more go out and come in; and
the Lord said unto me: Thou shalt not go over the Jordan.
The Lord, thy God, He will go over before thee. . . . And
Joshua, he shall go over before thee" (*Deuteronomy 31:1-3*).

As Moses assured his people that he would leave them
in the good care of both God and Joshua, we are told:
"And Moses went and spoke." Where did he go? Scripture leaves this open and does not tell us where he went.
The commentaries fill us in on this.

Dr. A. Cohen, in his notes to the Soncino Chumash
following the commentaries of Ibn Ezra, Nahmanides and
Sforno, writes: "After concluding his exhortation to the
whole assembly which then dispersed, Moses went from

tribe to tribe, to announce his approaching end, to comfort the people and encourage them to put their trust in his successor."

At this point in his life Moses did not call the people to come to him and to receive his message as he had been accustomed to doing, nor did he address himself to the whole congregation in general. He paid individual visits to each of them. Being intimately involved with his people over such a long period, he felt that his farewell from them required more than a public manifestation. In visiting each one, old-time memories surfaced and heart-to-heart dialogue ensued. It was heartwarming and reassuring for the people to be privileged with a personal visit by the "old man" himself. It certainly was not an easy chore for the aged Moses, but he must have considered it nevertheless worth the effort. Even in his last days, the kind and caring leader did not spare himself when the well-being of his flock was at stake.

Other commentators (*kli yakar, al ha-torah*) explain the phrase "And Moses went" to convey the simple fact that Moses actually moved around in his usual manner of walking. This is mentioned in order to underscore his statement which follows: "I can no more go out and come in." In spite of his one-hundred-twenty years, "Moses went" to show that he was indeed able to walk as swiftly and briskly as before. He wished to tell them that he was not retiring because of failing health due to old age, but that he could no longer "go out and come in" only because the Lord had said to him: "Thou shalt not go over the Jordan." As he complied with the wishes of the Lord, so must they. They must rest assured now that the Lord would be with them and with Joshua, their newly-appointed leader.

A less kind comment on the phrase "And Moses went" suggests that as soon as the people realized that Moses was really retiring, they ceased coming to him, so that in order to deliver his message he had to go and seek them out. Such is the way people treat their leaders as soon as they are out, or about to be out, of office. All those who had followed Moses as long as he was on top suddenly disappeared. Now they were probably busy trying to make connections with the incoming administration and had no time left to go and visit with Moses. Although he was about to leave office, he certainly had a thing or two to tell them, but they were not there to listen to him. Now he had to go and look for them.

Moses' message to the people and to Joshua consists of two parts. First, he reassures them that no leader is indispensable, especially in view of the fact that it was not he personally that deserved the credit for all the great and good things that happened to them, but the Almighty God who would continue to be with them. At the same time, he wishes to bring to their attention that it is not enough to rely on God alone to bring them to the Land. They cannot lean back passively and wait for God to conquer the Land for them. They must "be strong and of good courage."

This exhortation to "be strong and of good courage" is repeated several times, both here (31:6, 7) and in the book of Joshua (1: 6, 7, 18). It seemed to have become the slogan of the entire campaign for the conquest of the Land.

To inherit the Land of Israel one cannot rely merely on God, but one must possess two other qualities. First, to be strong; and second, to be of good courage. One without the other would not do. The might of the army, a large quantity of weapons, even the high sophistication of tanks and warplanes would not perform the job, if along with them there were not courage and the deep motivation of each and every commander and soldier. On the other hand, motivation and courage by themselves would not do the job either without a strong, well-equipped and well-trained army.

To this day, this remains the central idea and ideal of the *Zahal*, the Israel Defense Forces. The Israeli soldier is usually sworn in at a special solemn ceremony which takes place at a site selected for its historic associations in regard to the motivation of serving in a Jewish army following almost 2000 years of Jewish defenseless helplessness. The Western Wall in Jerusalem and the hilltop of Massada are two such locales. At the ceremony, which takes place in the presence of the members of the families and friends of the new soldiers, every recruit is called up by name and presented with a gun and a Bible. One is for "strength," the other for "good courage."

Pride and Prejudice

THE INSCRIPTION POSTED at the entrance to the Yad V'shem Holocaust Memorial in Jerusalem quotes the following saying from the writings of the great hassidic master Nahman of Bratslav: "In remembering is the secret of redemption." Torah, especially in the book of Deuteronomy, warns us over and over again "to remember" and "not to forget." Even in his last parting words, in the poetic formulation of his farewell address, Moses enjoins the people (*Deuteronomy 32:7*):

> Remember the days of old;
> Consider (understand) the generation long past.
> Ask your father and he will tell you,
> Your elders (grandfathers) and they will explain to you.

What is added here is that "remembering" historical facts is not enough; one must also reflect upon them, consider them in order to "understand" their meaning.

Torah would not agree necessarily with the wisdom of Plutarch that "history repeats itself." It does not. It is only we that repeat its failures as well as its achievements. Recalling the past and understanding it helps us put events into their proper focus. Even though we may think of ourselves as wise, resourceful, and technologically advanced, we are brought to realize that there is still much we can learn from our parents, and that even our grandparents have much that is worth sharing with us.

Long before Alex Haley succeeded in turning people's attention to learning about their "roots," Jews were keen on acknowledging the constructive pride to be derived from getting to know their roots. This pride was not aimed at inflating one's sense of importance or meant to encourage shallow conceit, nor was it meant to confer more privileges and status for the "blue-blooded" elite. On the contrary, it was reason for imposing more obligations and restrictions. There is a short, but very meaningful Yiddish expression that is invoked on such occasions: *s'paast nisht*. It does not suit a person of distinguished lineage. "A descendant of 'X' would not do such things."

Jewish tradition esteemed *yihus*, an impressive pedigree, but was also well aware of its dangers. *Noblesse oblige* could easily turn into *snoblesse oblige*. This happens when we forget that what we do is much more significant than who we are.

Our ancestors who made sure to teach us pride in our family roots also reminded us constantly that it is better to be the "first," rather than the "last," of a distinguished genealogical line. Parents and grandparents give us pride not only by hanging their portraits on the wall, but also by seeing to it that we acquire from them and from their lives guidance and values to improve our lives.

Modern times prevent many people from having close and immediate contact with their parents. We are witness to more than one "lost generation" in the direct chain of tradition. "Ask your father and he will tell you, your grandfathers and they will explain to you." At times when we do what Torah advises us to do, namely "Ask your father," we will find that what "he will tell you" is that "your grandfather will explain to you." Father still knows Jewish life from grandpa's house, but he no longer has the know-how to explain things to us; therefore he must refer us to grandfather. One should nevertheless ask—and create the opportunity to learn from "grandfather"—as some day we ourselves will be the grandparents. What shall we tell our grandchildren and how are we going to explain things to them?

Being proud and getting to know the roots of one's culture is not just a hobby or pastime, but a delicate and sophisticated business. Muki Zur, the kibbutz educator, tells about a person who, learning of the importance of roots, every morning would take out the sapling he had planted to check its roots. Of course, it never grew into a tree.

Benjamin Disraeli, Earl of Beaconsfield (1804-1881), was born a Jew and remained fiercely proud of his Jewish roots, although his family later left the fold. "Yes, I am a Jew," he replied 150 years ago to a taunt by a political opponent who chided him about being Jewish, "and when the ancestors of the right honourable gentleman were brutal savages on an unknown island, mine were priests in the Temple of Solomon."

Disraeli was not the only one in his times to defend proudly his Jewishness. In his *Reminiscenses of Sixty Years in the National Metropolis* (1886), Ben Perley Poore quotes this reply of United States Senator Judah P. Benjamin (1811-1884) to a senator of German extraction who taunted him with being a Jew: "The gentleman will please remember that when his half-civilized ancestors were hunting the wild boar in the forests of Silesia, mine were the princes of the earth."

Closer to our own time, a story is told about the famous

Reform rabbi Stephen Wise, who found himself seated at a gala dinner next to a pompous high-society lady who could not wait long before she announced to her neighbor that her ancestors "crossed the ocean and landed at Plymouth Rock." Wise politely expressed his admiration for the lady's ancestral lineage, adding calmly: "And my ancestors, dear lady, crossed the Red Sea and landed at Mount Sinai."

The worst tragedy, says hassidic master Aaron of Karlin, is when the prince forgets that he is a prince. Pride in one's roots is indeed a precious commodity. It is, however, a two-edged sword. When out of control, it could then become counter-productive. Torah enjoins us not only to "remember" the roots of the past, but—more important—to "understand" them.

The Last Blessing

THE VERY LAST ACT performed by Moses before his death was to confer a blessing on his people.

"And this is the blessing, wherewith Moses the man of God blessed the children of Israel before his death" (*Deuteronomy 33:1*). There follows a poetic address in which parts are directed to the Israelites as a whole and the rest to each and every tribe in particular.

Many were the epithets and titles given to Moses in the course of his long career. Now, close to his death, is the first time and the last that he is referred to as *ish ha-elohim,* "man of God." I believe that he was called this not to emphasize his relationship to God, but rather to underscore his remaining "man" even now. Being closer to God than ever before and about to leave this mundane world to embrace eternity, Moses was not concentrating only on himself, pondering his life in preparation to meet his Maker. His attention, even at this moment, was given to blessing the children of Israel. Intoxicated with godliness, he remains nevertheless to his very last breath, a man among men, a human being preserving that precious quality which is represented by the untranslatable Yiddish expression—to be *"a mentsch."*

In his blessing, Moses (just like his great-grandfather Jacob did prior to his death) does not lump all the people together when blessing them. The blessings are custom-made, tailored for each one of the tribes and relating to their particular history and characteristics.

When the act of blessing is finished, Moses went up to the top of Mount Nebo to take a last look at the Land towards which he devoted his life and led his people and which, alas, he himself was not going to see. Torah does not tell us what his reaction was upon seeing the land from afar. Did he like what he saw? Was he satisfied at the bird's-eye view of the land unfolding in front of his eyes? Was he still bitter about his personal inability to get there? Not a word is uttered to let us know the answer to these questions. Moses, so absorbed in the sights, apparently turned speechless. All we know is that God, who serves as his "tour guide" at that moment, does not select a partial itinerary in order for him to see only certain "interesting" sites, but He showed him *all* the land (*ibid.*, 34: 1-3), "even Gilead as far as Dan, and all of Naphtali, and the land of Ephraim, and all the land of Judah, as far as the hinder sea, and the South, and the Plain, even the valley of Jericho, the city of palm trees, as far as Zoar." What an intensive tour! Now that the entire land was indelibly inscribed on Moses' mind, he could die peacefully.

"So Moses, the servant of the Lord died there in the land of Moab, according to the word (*al pi ha-shem*— literally by the mouth) of the Lord" (*verse 5*). The rabbis (and Rashi on the spot) explained this as meaning that Moses died by the Divine Kiss, *mitat neshika*. The Divine Kiss, which made Moses' death painless and peaceful, was the sight of Eretz Israel which hovered before his eyes at that moment.

Moses was not the only Jewish leader who went to his eternal rest with the memory and presence of the Holy Land on his mind. There is an old custom practiced by

many Jews who live *hutz la-aretz,* outside of Israel, to keep
a precious little bag of earth from the Holy Land available
so that it can be spread over their eyes right after returning their last breath to their Maker.

The sights and vistas of Eretz Israel always accompanied Jews both in their lives and their death even while
being far away from the Land. Some landscape of the
Holy Land, in painting or embroidery was always a desirable decoration in the Jewish Home. Some would leave a
blank square on the wall as a constant reminder of Jerusalem being missed and remembered with love.

Abraham Moshe Luntz, one of the early experts in the
modern study of Israel in the past century, specialized in
the history and geography of the Land, particularly Jerusalem. He was a notable scholar and edited close to fifty
(!) books on the subject, most of them still valuable
today—a hundred years later. Luntz was also a tour guide
for distinguished visitors to Jerusalem, happily sharing
with them the rich treasures of his knowledge and love of
the city. As he turned twenty-five years old, Luntz was
told by the doctors that he was stricken with a serious eye
ailment (which was very common in Jerusalem during
those years) and that he would surely lose his eyesight
shortly. They advised him to go abroad for surgery that
might save his eyesight. Before embarking on his journey
to Vienna for the operation, Luntz spent ten days on the
rooftops of Jerusalem, absorbing all the views of the city
which he knew so well and loved so much. Returning
from Vienna six months later following unsuccessful surgery and completely blind, Luntz continued for another
fifty years to write his books and conduct tours of the city
for visitors. He, the blind man, would *show* and explain
every street and alley, every nook and cranny which he
would see constantly, not with the eyes of the flesh but of
the spirit. People would marvel at this "John Milton" of
Jerusalem, carrying around the "paradise" he never lost

even after losing his sight and only then understand the Hebrew-Aramaic euphemism for the blind, "*sagi nahor,*" meaning "full of light." He lost his sight, not his vision.

AFTER THIRTY days of mourning (*Deuteronomy 34:8*) (this, by the way, is the source of the *shloshim,* the thirty days of mourning for a death in Jewish tradition), Joshua steps in as the leader to implement the great tasks which lie ahead of the people—to conquer and inherit the Land.

Torah testifies regarding the new leader that "Joshua, the son of Nun, was full of the spirit of wisdom" (*verse 9*) and ready for the responsible job. His wisdom was perhaps expressed mainly in the statement that follows: "and there has not arisen in Israel since then a prophet like Moses." Joshua in his wisdom realized that although he took over the job of Moses, he would never be like Moses nor could he ever fill his shoes.

The larger miracle was, however, in the fact that "the children of Israel hearkened" unto Joshua. Yes, there were those who complained that by comparison Joshua was much smaller than Moses and that when one compared the two, one would appear like the sun, the other like the moon. Nevertheless, "the children of Israel hearkened." They understood that Moses was no longer with them and that comparing the present-day leaders with the giants of the past was unfair and non-realistic.

Joshua also had to be reminded not to try to be Moses and to be just himself, Joshua. Thus his own book in the Bible starts with the Lord speaking to Joshua, saying to him: "My servant Moses is dead." Did not Joshua know that? Of course he knew, but he had to be made aware of the fact, that one cannot go back, nor yearn for the leadership of Moses. Moses is dead and "now it is for you to cross the Jordan, you and this whole people of Israel, to the land which I am giving them."

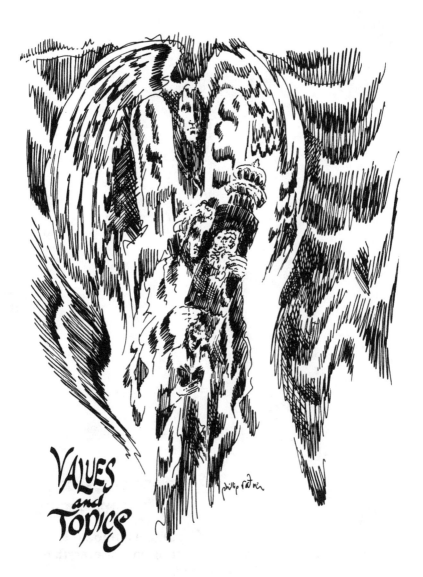

VALUES
and
TOPICS

philip ratner

כֶּן-בַּג בַּג אוֹמֵר, הֲפָךְ-בָּהּ
וְהַפָךְ-בָּהּ דְּכֹלָּא-בָהּ

Ben Bag Bag said: Turn to it [Torah]
over and over again, for everything
is contained in it,

Chapters of Fathers 5, 26

Guide to Values and Topics